WILLEM LAMMERS

PHRASES to FREEDOM

Self-Coaching with Logosynthesis

Copyright ©2009, Willem Lammers, 7304 Maienfeld,
Switzerland
Translated by Patricia Cooney

ISBN: 1-4392-4788-9
ISBN 13: 9781439247884

Copyright notice:
Logosynthesis is a trademark of Willem Lammers, CH-7304
Maienfeld.
No part of this publication may be reproduced and/ or
distributed in any form without prior written permission of the
author.

Visit *www.booksurge.com* to order additional copies.

To my Clients

Contents

Foreword

Learning is a lifelong process. We are developing—in body, mind, and spirit. As we mature and grow older, our physical capabilities diminish. In the course of our journey, we encounter obstacles, again and again, causing benefits or damages. The path never runs smooth or level. Even when it seems direct, our fate meets with the unexpected.

Over the years, as a psychologist and coach, I had sought to discover the essence of personal transformation and development. Then I chanced upon a minor miracle—the miracle of words. Subsequently, the many elements of my thirty years' practice formed a cohesive unit as Logosynthesis. The jigsaw puzzle of my experience pieced together into a fascinating, unified picture.

Words perform miracles. Logosynthesis became an enthralling, elegant model employing a surprisingly effective method. Using Logosynthesis you will find solutions to everyday questions and gain mastery over many aspects of your life. The method will enable you to:

- *Take control of your own life*
- *Identify and achieve your goals in life*
- *Form more dynamic and positive relationships*
- *Free up the energy to enjoy life*
- *Enhance your performance, efficiency, and satisfaction at work.*

In short, you will learn how to release yourself from what you no longer desire and achieve what you really want. Logosynthesis will basically allow you to transform your life.

This book is dedicated to those who have shown confidence in me over the past thirty years. My work with them as coach, psychotherapist, and teacher formed the basis of Logosynthesis. I am deeply grateful.

My thanks also to Anna Seraina Arquint, Pat Esborg, Henny van Laarhoven, Ria Lammers, Beate Kircher, Nancy Porter-Steele, Curtis Steele, Peter Vinzenz, Gabi Zindel, and Beat Zindel for their comments on the manuscript. They have contributed a great deal to the final draft of this book. I especially want to thank Patricia Cooney for the English translation.

My previous book *Logosynthesis – Change through the Magic of Words* was aimed at professionals in the fields of coaching, counselling, and psychotherapy. It placed Logosynthesis within the theoretical and methodological tradition of guided change against the background of an integral understanding of Man's existence. When that book was published, many individuals asked how they could learn to use Logosynthesis for self-help and personal healing. This book fulfils that purpose. It does not claim to provide an answer to every question or preclude counselling, coaching, or psychotherapy under a trained professional. On the contrary, at turning points in our lives, it is better to place our trust in the treatment, experience, and skill of trained professionals. In any case, this book is intended to introduce Logosynthesis as a magical tool for personal development and healing.

In this volume, I should like to provide you with a basic understanding of Logosynthesis as a model and a method of personal coaching. You will release yourself—your true self—from emotional wounds, self-limiting thinking, and outmoded patterns of behaviour. You will not discover all the answers today, but today you can begin.

Maienfeld, in the summer of 2009,

Willem Lammers

1.
Introduction

January 11, 2005 marks the definitive starting point for Logosynthesis. In my consulting room, I saw a woman named Leonore. She was about forty-five years of age, and suffering from a variety of complaints following a curious fall down the stairs of a railway station six years earlier. She could barely remember what had happened at the time. All she knew was that she was injured in the fall as she tried to board a train.

During our session, I discovered, bit by bit, that she was living in two separate spatial positions of her Self. In her Swiss dialect, she used the idiom "beside my shoes" and told me how that morning she had misjudged the position of the shower door when she had reached for it. Just at that moment, I noticed a kind of shadow to the right of her body. I was captivated by this sequence of evidence, and decided to take her at her word, "beside my shoes." I shared my thoughts with her and asked her to try to unite the two parts I perceived. She succeeded at the second attempt. We were both surprised at the very strong emotions this brought up for her, and after about ten minutes, she was able to describe what had taken place six years previously—how she had been knocked off her feet that fatal morning, fallen down the stairs, and remained lying on the cold concrete floor.

I was astonished by this discovery. After our session, I began to research the dynamic principles behind the happening. I found that what people consider to be the Self may become fragmented, and that such fragments can even occupy various positions in space. I also discovered that within each individual's personal space, there are representations of people and things, and that people react to those representations as if they were really, physically present.

To me, the concept was an exciting one. In time, I sought the underlying principles behind my observations. I also found that saying specific sentences can repair inner fragmentation. These discoveries led to a fully evolved healing system, which I called Logosynthesis—"integration through the word."

I began to explore the application of Logosynthesis in my work as a coach and psychotherapist. At this moment, just a few years on, these beginnings have grown into an integral system of coaching and development in which I have instructed many colleagues in counselling, coaching, and psychotherapy.

1.1.
What Is Logosynthesis?

"Everything flows, nothing stands still"

– HERACLITUS

Put aside everything you ever learnt about change, for just a few days. That is what I suggest to my colleagues who learn Logosynthesis. I am giving you the same advice, readers. Put aside your knowledge and experience for just a hundred pages. Everything may be quite different to what you thought until now. Take up a new starting point. It will not be entirely new, but it represents a fresh combination of ideas.

Did you get this book to learn something new? Or, was it to confirm your previous insights? If it was to consolidate your own ideas, then ask yourself why you need it. Why don't you have confidence in your own judgement? Here we are in right in the middle of Logosynthesis. One part of you is sceptical about new ideas, while another clearly longs for them. There are two sides to everyone, and during your life, both sides are often the same. This was known as early as in the time of Goethe, who wrote in Faust:

"Alas, two souls live in my breast…"

There are more than two aspects of the psyche—there are hundreds, even thousands. Through the ages, man has sought to understand himself and his souls. Every day we are involved in internal dialogues about minor issues. We ask ourselves:

- *Will I get up now or turn over again?*
- *Do I save this money or spend it?*
- *Will I stay home or go out?*
- *Should I have another cigarette?*
- *Will I have dessert as well?*
- *Will I watch more television or go to bed?*

Important issues lead us to deeper internal debates such as:

- *Which school should I go to?*
- *What job do I take?*
- *Which one of the two do I love more?*
- *Should I get married?*
- *Do I want another child?*
- *Should I change jobs?*
- *Should I get a divorce?*
- *Should I retire early?*
- *Who will inherit in my will?*

This inner debate goes on and on. Have you been in a situation where you tried to make a decision for ages, then one day the answer just seemed to come to you? You needn't have put all that energy into it—it was so simple. A higher internal authority showed you the path and the dilemma was solved. The dilemma, the double-edge ended. You simply got to the heart of the matter and found a higher clarity, a superior truth. But how did you discover this clarity, your own truth? A lot of us search our innermost Self, while others among us talk things over with their partner or friends. Some throw coins for an I Ching oracle or have their cards read. More seek professional help from a coach or psychotherapist or perhaps an astrologer. Whichever route you take to seek out your own truth, it is your deepest personal truth. When you have come upon it, you will see this. Any means or helpers will seem to have just opened a window into this self-evident truth. How will you recognise your own truth? Try this exercise for a few minutes:

Think of a decision that was important to you and which you can look back on later with satisfaction. You knew then and you know now you made the right choice. Answer the following questions:

- *How did I reach this decision?*
- *Did I look for help or assistance?*
- *What were the stages in my decision-making process?*
- *How did I finally reach a decision?*
- *How did I recognise this as exactly the right alternative?*
- *What physical sensations did I experience at the moment of recognition?*

If you repeat this exercise for some of your good decisions, you will notice the same every time. Within yourself, there is an authority that knows what is right regardless of how you reached the decision. *When your friend told you what you ought to do, you knew inside yourself that it was right. Meditation was illuminating. When that special Tarot card faced up you sensed its meaning.* Who or what showed you the answer? It wasn't your friend or the card. It was your Self. It was the manifestation of your innermost Being, your higher Self, your Essence, as Ali Hameed Almaas called it.

In this book, I will use Almaas' term *Essence* for the power beyond space and time from which material existence is manifested. I will refer to this individual manifestation of Essence as the *Self*.

You are more than your physical body, but your body is part of you. Your body is the vehicle, the means of transport, which helps you to move about freely in the world. Your senses show you the world. You are also more than a mind. Your mind, your worldly ego, cannot elevate your existence to a higher meaning. Its workings are limited by the world, intuition, and logic.

Essence manifested as your Self, is wiser. You become familiar with these qualities as soon as you make the right decision—your profound personal truth, knowledge beyond space and time. This knowledge means you don't need other people to confirm that you're right. It endures beyond the present moment and pervades your entire life. From Ken Wilber, I adapted the following diagram, which represents this concept of the world:

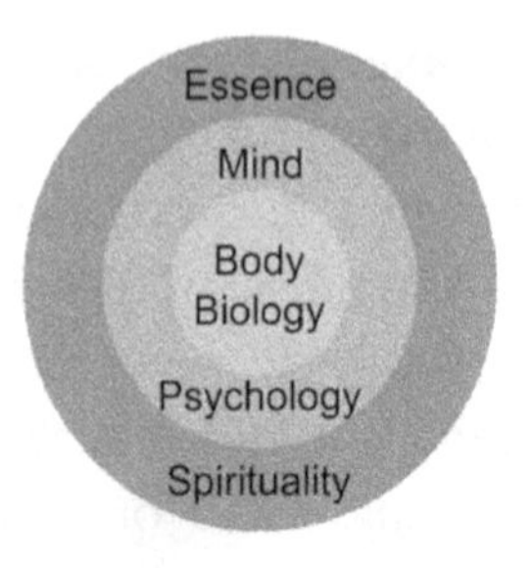

Franz Kafka refers to Essence as "the Indestructible" in contrast to all worldly things that may die, be lost, or break into pieces. Knowledge of Essence will also give you insight into your deepest motives. Life experience also is experience of this Essence. In the course of their lives, many people find access to this Essence—by falling and getting back up again. Logosynthesis is a quicker, easier way to come to this inner knowledge and become more familiar with your own Essence.

Logosynthesis alleviates human suffering and facilitates personal growth. It contains a model, guidelines for change, and practical methods based on a coherent view of the person. The term is composed of two ancient Greek words that are well recognised in our own culture: *logos* is Greek for "meaning," "sense," "mind," or "doctrine." In Logosynthesis, it stands for both "meaning" and "word." The Greek word *synthesis* means "to bring together" or "to come together" and refers to the integration of the various parts of the personality into the Living Self. "Bringing together" can also be interpreted as "making whole" or "healing," thus, Logosynthesis may also be translated word-for-word as "healing through words." It is no coincidence that the term may remind you of Viktor Frankl's Logotherapy (1987) and Roberto Assagioli's Psychosynthesis (1993). Frankl's concept is governed by three basic philosophical and psychological principles:

- The freedom of will
- The will for meaning
- The meaning of life

Viktor Frankl is credited as being among the first to expand psychotherapy to include the spiritual dimension. Robert Assagioli, the founder of Psychosynthesis, similarly took the interaction of body, mind, and spirit as a given.

The model of Logosynthesis provides a simple but comprehensive explanation for human suffering. The principles of change, and the method, will show you how you can reduce your own and other people's suffering. Because of its simplicity, the model often meets resistance; opponents ask, "Can the answer to such a broad question be so simple?" Yes, it can. The practical application is somewhat less simple. Even with the help of Logosynthesis, it is difficult to create a new order in your life experience with its uplifting and harsh experiences. It is difficult even when it is meant to alleviate your suffering, but it is worthwhile every day. You will notice the difference from the start, and you can monitor your development closely. Both the model and the method are astonishingly simple. They can be that simple because they understand and deal with human suffering from its roots.

People are body, mind, and spirit—biological, sociopsychological, and spiritual beings. These aspects of our existence are related and not really separable. They're aspects of the same higher reality. Differentiating them, however, helps us to examine our lives, especially when one of them is causing a problem for us. Change can take place on every level, but change processes are most effective when the processes on the levels of body, mind, and soul complement each other. Logosynthesis proposes a model for understanding human beings on three levels: the biological, the psychological, and the spiritual. We can compare these levels with working on a computer:

- Biology focuses on elementary survival in the Earth Life System. Through the senses, our organism receives input from the environment. Through the body, we react in a way this organisme can survive: feed, fight, flight, and procreation. This aspect corresponds to the computer hardware—the screen, the keyboard, and the processor.
- Our psychology contains the ability of our mind to shape our lives actively in our physical environment, in our relationships, in our work, and in society. We can compare this to the computer software—programmes for word processing, spreadsheet calculation, and presentation. In a similar fashion, we have programmes for living.
- Our spirituality adds meaning to the tasks of body and mind, along with a higher purpose. We can compare this aspect of our existence with the computer operator. He decides what he will use his computer for and which programme to start. When his work is over, he'll switch it off.

DIALOGUE

In applying Logosynthesis, we learn to reconnect with our Essence and to heal the split between body, mind and spirit. A great number of self-help books and websites give advice in a slightly contradictory way like this:

- *Accept yourself as you are.*
- *Seek security within yourself, not from outside.*
- *Let criticism roll off you.*
- *Don't take everything personally.*
- *Learn to say "no."*

Advice like this assumes that you have an inner certainty, like an internal voice, and that you can solve your problems by listening to this voice. However, if you don't hear this sure inner voice or feel unable to listen to it, you're in trouble. Inevitably, you will have to listen to external voices to find that security you need. Usually, various inner voices are negotiating with the external ones. That's fine because if you only listen to your internal voices, you'll lose touch with the world, whereas if you only listen to the external ones, there won't be much of your own Self left. In the course of their lives, many people lose the ability to tell the difference between internal and external voices. This is where Logosynthesis comes in:

- Logosynthesis recognises several types of inner voices. It will develop your skills to learn the difference between them. You will gain a higher awareness of what's essential in your life.
- It will also show you how to find these essential aspects in difficult situations and use them as vantage points, without relying too much on voices from the outside.
- Logosynthesis will help you to separate the voices of your past from those in the present and, thus, assure the future.

If you consistently follow the guidelines in this book, you can use Logosynthesis to clarify many aspects of your life.

In the following chapter, I will introduce you to the four basic principles behind Logosynthesis. These form the basis necessary to understand the model of the world described earlier. They are also at the heart of Logosynthesis as a means of changing physical symptoms, emotions, thought processes, and beliefs. It will further your development on your innermost personal level. I will explain the method and then show you small examples of how the method can also work for you. By working on small issues, you will build up to a routine, which will allow you to initiate big changes in the long run. If you need help on this, there are a growing number of trained experts in coaching, counselling, and psychotherapy who can guide you on the road to change. If you start to work with Logosynthesis, it is important that you follow the guidelines and formulations given in this book exactly as they're written.

The method of Logosynthesis is derived directly from four theses. It has proved itself in daily practice, but for the time being, we cannot expect scientific evidence of its application. For the model, there's no reference to the current scientific paradigm. Therefore, the application of the model also differs from other psychological and psychotherapeutic methods on a fundamental level.

The model and techniques are so straightforward that some people cannot believe that they will work at all. They start making up their own variations of the method. They adapt them to more conventional, rational ways of thinking, even before they have tried to apply it in the way described in this book. Such experiments go beyond the working principles of Logosynthesis, and can even disturb the healing process. A great number of people underestimate the power of saying *just* a sentence without emphasis or emotion, neither adding conscious intention nor thinking about it. They don't see how this sentence can initiate change at the deepest level or bring relief from suffering. The best way to understand Logosynthesis is by practising the technique for yourself.

Previous methods and models of change were based mainly on either physical, psychological, energetic, or spiritual principles. They complemented one another in relatively few cases. Similarly, many current theories and methods are based on a single perspective and exclude others. Thus, suffering and resolution are interpreted alternatively as physical, mental, energetic, or spiritual and the process of change is initiated on the basis chosen.

Physically orientated models perceive suffering as somatic and neurological. These create change through medication, diet, or physical exercise. Psychological models produce change by altering our thoughts, feelings, and behaviours. They draw on the psychoanalytic and humanistic schools or on Cognitive Behavioural Therapy. Energy Psychology views suffering as a blockage in the energy flow, and restores the flow through breathing techniques—or perhaps by stimulating chakras and acupuncture points. Spiritual methods consider suffering to be a lack of awareness and operate through prayer, meditation, dance, or Tantra. Logosynthesis works from the common roots of these models. It takes a separate and unique stance, which takes some time to become familiar with, but which will become clear easily while practicing. To summarise briefly, Logosynthesis

- is an integrative developmental system, which will help us to reconnect to our true Being and, thus, relieve suffering;
- comprises a model and a method;

- combines current psychotherapeutic concepts and Energy Psychology with ancient healing knowledge;
- restarts the free flow of energy between Essence and the Earth Life System through the power of the Word
- can not only be used for coaching, counselling, and psychotherapy, but also for personal and spiritual development; and
- has a broad range of applications, for example, fears, phobias, compulsive disorders, and the processing of traumatic events—it can also dispel blocking beliefs and obstacles to a fulfilled life and career, as well as health problems and relationship issues.

2.
The Four Axioms

"Nowadays the mental-spiritual approach is in danger of being suppressed by the materialist perspective. The same applies to current professional trends in psychiatry and psychology. Without a dualistic approach, the person is emotionally stunted, and eventually questions himself. Since he is reduced to an object of scrutiny and a "data carrier," he loses sight of what ultimately makes him human."

– DANIEL HELL

THE FOUR KEY AXIOMS

Logosynthesis is founded on four principles, theses, or axioms. I will introduce them in this book, but not discuss them in depth, even though each axiom might constitute a lengthy heated debate among authorities in the fields of philosophy, theology, psychology, and physics. Concerning Logosynthesis, the four axioms constitute a starting point for a way of seeing the world. They also are the key to its application as a tool for development and change.

The four principles encompass the human being, the nature of suffering, and the necessary means of alleviating such suffering. Together the principles form a complete concept. The number of theses has been reduced to the absolute minimum, and this minimum makes for power and elegance. Logosynthesis can't be properly understood without each of these four axioms. We need them all to describe our goals and the obstacles on our path, and to determine how to dissolve our obstacles. All the methods of problem-solving, relief from suffering, and growth described in this book derive from the combination of the four axioms. They can explain all the healing processes people have gone through in working with Logosynthesis. The combination of the four axioms is sufficient to understand healing and personal growth. More than these four would detract from Logosynthesis. For most readers, these theses will be more or less familiar. The four axioms are:

1. The true Self does not suffer. Suffering originates from a lack of awareness of Essence and our purpose in this world.
2. Awareness of our true Self is reduced or impeded by dissociation (splitting off parts of consciousness) and introjection (the representation of people and objects inside our body and personal space).
3. Dissociated parts and introjects—also called imprints—are frozen energy structures in multidimensional space and not simply abstract concepts.
4. The power of the Word will dissolve these frozen structures and free Life Energy for our true task in space and time.

Open yourself for these principles and discover how you can apply Logosynthesis for yourself!

2.1.

Axiom 1. The True Self Does Not Suffer

"When you are inspired by a higher goal,
a new project,
your thoughts will exceed the boundaries.
Dormant powers, skills and talents come to life
and you discover that you are greater
than you ever dared to dream."

– PATANJALI

THE FIRST KEY AXIOM

The true Self does not suffer. Suffering originates from a lack of awareness of Essence and our task in this world.

EXERCISE: RIGHT NOW, ALL IS WELL

Find a peaceful place and relax. Breathe deeply in and out several times. With each outward breath repeat the word "relax" until you sense a deep relaxation in your limbs...now imagine going back in time time...recall a time or times when all your Life Energy was at your disposal, when you felt: "Yes, at this moment, all is well."

Recall this situation to your conscious mind, along with the thoughts, emotions, and physical sensations. Examine the situation more closely:

- When was it?
- Where was it?
- Who was present?
- How did my body feel?
- Which emotions was I aware of?

People who do this exercise often say that it was as if time stood still. Their personal needs disappeared into the background. The past and the future seemed to have lost their meaning. Only the here-and-now was important, as well as the people who were right there with them. Their feelings alternated between love and gratitude. Fear, shame, dislike, rage, and anger all seemed to disappear. It was as if there was communication without words.

Axiom I assumes that a human being is an Essence that transcends life in this world. It differs from the usual biological unity of body and mind, which holds that the human body originates from the fertilised egg cell and that, equally, the mind has its origins in the fertilised egg cell. From this point of view, the individual is subject to two types of influence: heredity and environment, or *nature* and *nurture*.

Logosynthesis takes the view that we are more than a physical body trying to survive on this earth and pass on our genes. We are more than a mind consciously trying to achieve our goals. We are greater.

THE BODY

We are a body, a physical body with the needs of the physical world—eating, drinking, belonging, avoiding danger, and desiring to reproduce. The entire existence of the earthly body is dedicated to the function of biological *survival*. We seek to survive as an individual and a species.

Biology and Medicine examine this body using empirical methods—as matter, as a machine, or as the interaction of matter and energy. Scientific methodology does not recognise a fundamental difference between humans, animals. and plants.

THE MIND

Together with a body, we also have a mind. Through our senses, we collect information from the environment and react to it. We are adaptable. We can handle rain and dryness, heat and cold, within limits. We have a further physical and mental capacity to alter our environment actively and organise it in almost any way we please. In addition, we process and combine our sense impressions of our surroundings. We can form personal and collective goals and devote our energy to achieving them in time and space. We can explore the mind with rational means. Scientific psychology explores processes in individuals, and sociology focuses on groups in the context of society.

ESSENCE

We are even more than that. Since the beginning of man's history, an Essence—a higher self, a true self, an inspirational deity—forms part of our human experience. We are beings beyond time and space, continuously in the process of development. We are capable of actively organising our world based on creative intention. The world always assumes the form necessary for the continuously growing awareness of Essence. Our life has meaning and creates meaning. This viewpoint defies scientific explanation. Such knowledge is found only within ourselves. It may be known exclusively within, and expressed by, the individual. External observations cannot truly access its contents.

A scan of the temporal lobe of the brain of a person praying reveals as little information about the experience as the magnetic properties of my computer's hard drive reveals about the book that I am storing right now. We can, nevertheless, access Essence in various ways. There are the classic methods like meditation, mysticism, and contemplation. They are not, however, the only ones. Loving relationships, dreams, art, culture, work, dancing, sports, or, equally, counselling, coaching, and psychotherapy can open a window or a door to the awareness of Essence.

THE TASK

Essence marks the difference between a living and a dead body, between the psyche and a computer. Essence changes the naked ape into a human being and provides him with a task for his life, a task that brings meaning and significance. Everyone comes into this world with a unique mission and the potential to fulfil this mission, to master this task, and with the potential to be a human being. In the beginning of our lives, we are our *Original Self*, in touch with our true nature. Then, we know that we are, in reality:

- immortal,
- invulnerable, and
- omnipotent.

Our most profound Self is neither male nor female, and it knows nothing of age. In the Earth Life System, we cannot preserve this awareness for long. Soon after we arrive on the Earth, we have a bumpy landing. At the start of our lives, we're aware of Essence, but we don't know bodily needs, have no language, and can't understand the world around us. It is impossible to preserve this awareness of Essence. The evidence is too strong that everything is different in this world.

- We are growing in a sac that is getting too small in the final phase of pregnancy. The passage through the birth canal is painful, and not all of us are heartily welcomed.
- After birth, the body is sensitive to hunger and pain and restricted in its freedom of movement.
- The mind's capacity to understand people and the environment is extremely limited.
- We have physical and emotional needs we don't understand.
- We can express these needs only through crying in different ways.
- These can only be fulfilled by someone else who understands them
- The transience of the body will soon become apparent.

THE SELF AS LIVING ESSENCE

Despite this difficult start in the Earth Life System, the awareness of Essence, of the true Self beyond body and mind, is never totally lost. The Self as a living Essence is a flexible, creative, and dynamic system that can act freely in the here-and-now within the limits of the Earth Life System. It is a starting point for our individual mission, the work on our unique task in this life. Only the Self can give meaning to our existence in our physical bodies. Of course, others will want us to meet their needs and desires. But if we adapt to them without questioning if the others' needs mirror our mission, we are distancing ourselves from Essence. In his research into consciousness, the American researcher Charles T. Tart wrote in the context of learning in and on the body:

I think we are living this embodied life for a purpose,
a purpose that has something to do with learning,
learning knowledge, and more importantly, learning to love.

Disembodied states are wonderful in some ways,
but awfully vague in other ways, making it hard to learn some things.

A physical body provides focus, a stable platform for
learning so that the mind, the essence, the soul–whatever
we call it–is modified by the learning and growth this
body facilitates.

The position "right now, all is well," is the original position of the Self and the compass for our existence. Physical needs and psychic effort lose their importance, because being in contact with the Self is a source of deep harmony, even in adverse circumstances. There is a connection between the timeless Self and its physical/mental manifestation. It is the flow of energy, information, and awareness. This connection takes the form of pictures, symbols, physical experiences, emotions, fantasies, memories, or actions. Life Energy is visible in many forms. According to Eric Berne, it can be available in each of three manifestations: *free, bound,* or *potential* energy.

- Our *free energy* contributes to the fulfilment of our life task. When you are in touch with your free energy, you know within yourself your purpose in life. Your life task unfolds before you. You can choose effortlessly from among the broad range of options that confront you in everyday life in this world. You can opt for what is right for you and brings you a step further on your path in life. You can follow this path and further your interests without disregard for other people. The position of free-flowing energy puts you in touch effortlessly with courage, clarity, generosity, patience, wisdom, understanding, sympathy, certainty, humility, and joy. You have many resources to draw on and it affords the experience of love and profound gratitude.
- *Bound energy* is the opposite of free energy and has only one purpose: to stabilise your life through patterns. Bound energy stabilises your identity, perceptions, thoughts, and actions. You know who you are and you know what is expected of you. Stability brings peace

when it is associated with positive affect. Such peace is, however, deceptive because you are not really making any existential progress. Your days are predictable and there is no development. In this way, bound energy can impede or delay the fulfilment of your life mission. Energy is bound by limiting, blocking, or even destructive beliefs. This will cause stereotyped physical and affective patterns.

- *Potential energy* is energy that is not yet flowing, but can be released at a relatively low cost. This is the situation where you have really shed old burdens, but you still don't know where the journey will lead.

Our energy flow governs life and death. When our Life Energy stops flowing completely, life ends. The chemical composition of a living cell is not distinguishable from a dead one. There is only a single difference; in a living cell, an enormous number of chemical reactions are taking place to facilitate growth and development; in a dead cell, there is also chemical action, but here it splits the cell into its molecular and atomic components.

DEVELOPMENT

Our development predicts our energy flow—especially in early childhood. Our circumstances during this period of development influence the degree of freedom of our Life Energy. It also forecasts if and how our consciousness of Essence will remain intact. A baby must find a language for the storm of images, sounds, and feelings that assault his senses. He must do the same for his physical needs and for his experience of his physical and psychological boundaries.

In a meaningful social environment, newborns acquire language for the unexpected and often disagreeable events that occur in this world. Human society helps the original Self to construct internal representations of the world. Contact with the essential higher qualities remains unbroken. The child's ideal transition into the world is described in the famous Indian medicine text *Bhava Prakasuka*:

> *The yet unborn child is a god-like being. Thus, parents may not consider their own lives as the main focus. Furthermore, they should avoid fear and any sort of excitement, physical or mental. The parents are meant to use their body and soul to prepare a suitable place for the god-like being to live. They must consider their personal and family life themselves as an oasis with a godly atmosphere. It should be filled with calm and stillness, joy and delight. If they fulfil their responsibility in this way, the child will be, here in this world himself, in his true home. The child will be further filled with Satchitananda, pure being, consciousness, and blissful happiness. His consciousness will know unlimited peace and continue to enjoy Heaven's blessing in his mother's womb.*

In our society, reality is usually tougher. Even the best parents are sometimes overwhelmed by the balancing act between the child's needs, their own wishes, and the material and economic demands coming from the environment.

If parents are overwhelmed, their children cannot understand the world. Suffering is the result:

- The awareness of Essence, his own true Self and its task, is limited or lost. The child's experience is now based on his experience in mind and body.
- Both body and mind will suffer immediately if there is not enough food, heat, security, attention, or variety. The young child depends on people in the environment to eliminate the cause of such deficits. He doesn't have the means to do this for himself. Thus, he will give up his omnipotence and invulnerability and project them into the outside world.
- For his security, the child must depend on insecure caregivers. This increases his suffering further. The environment proves equally inadequate in fulfilling his needs in the Earth Life System. Initially the child will try to achieve the fulfilment of his needs, using the means available to him. He can only cry, and if that doesn't succeed, he will simply cry louder. If his parents neglect or ignore him, it will soon lead to passivity and resignation.

If an awareness of the Original Self cannot be preserved, something must occur if the person is not to lose the will to live completely. This brings us to the second principle of Logosynthesis. The person will adapt to the Earth Life System through dissociation and introjection.

2.2.
Axiom 2: Splitting and Introjection

"We tend to accept that the world is as we see it
and we naively assume that people are as we imagine them.
Thus we each create a series of imaginary relationships
that are essentially based on projections."

– C.G.JUNG

THE SECOND KEY AXIOM

Our awareness of Essence is reduced or hindered by splitting and introjection.

The second axiom of Logosynthesis describes what happens when our Original Self cannot assimilate our experiences of the world at the time when there is no one else present to support us in coming to terms with, or processing, such experiences.

The process of adaptation to the day-to-day reality of the Earth Life System can be described in terms of two interconnected phenomena: splitting and introjection. These concepts have been recognised since the beginning of the twentieth century; Pierre Janet and Sigmund Freud identified them for the first time. Carl Gustav Jung also considered that psychological problems could be divided into two basic categories, which he called splitting and possession. Since then, volumes have been written about these concepts, redefining them again and again. In this book, I will develop a specific view of these well-known phenomena.

ADAPTATION TO THE WORLD

The Original Self can only exist in this world through an extremely complex process of adaptation. I have described above the requirements for constructive development. They are seldom completely fulfilled. If the emotional and cognitive support coming from the environment is insufficient or lacking, the person is forced to reduce the complexity of his surroundings in another way. The Original Self utilises two closely connected mechanisms to adapt to the world:

1. Splitting, also called dissociation or fragmentation
2. Introjection

The awareness that our personality doesn't always operate consistently has been around for a long time. A famous quotation from Goethe's "Faust" states:

You are aware of only one desire,

O never learn of the other!

Two souls live, alas! in my breast,

One wants to separate from the other;

One follows, with intense desire,
this world with clinging organs;
The other rises powerfully from obscurity
to the realms of higher spirits.

SPLITTING OR DISSOCIATION

When the child meets the world, his Original Self cannot manage the pains and injuries of daily life as a human being, and parts of the Original Self are split off from awareness. Fragmentation develops—on the one hand, there is the Original Self with its awareness of its omnipotence and invulnerability; on the other hand, painful and incomprehensible experiences are stored as separate parts of consciousness, out of touch with Essence. They are stored as parts, of the body and the mind. This phenomenon is known as dissociation and has two main forms. In the first, people construct parts, which repress pain and allow them to progress somehow in the world—*the Apparently Normal Personality.* The Apparently Normal Personality is important. It can create a somewhat tolerable environment. We must adapt to the outside world so that our physical and psychological needs are fulfilled. The personality can create its own reality, dream, or fantasy world in order to repress painful psychic contents.

The second form of splitting creates parts where painful experiences are stored—*the Emotional Personality.* The split parts of the Emotional Personality are rooted in biological survival mechanisms: fear, rage, anger, disgust, and resignation. When these parts are activated, a person cannot tell the difference between the past and the present.

They can only utilise established patterns of thought and behaviour.

Both types of dissociated parts have lost immediate contact with awareness of the individual's Essence and meaning in life. They are split off as a reaction to traumatic or distressing events in the outside world or within the body. The Original Self cannot assimilate them. This process is intensified if there is no "good enough mother" to support the small child in processing his experiences in the world. The following functions can be split off as fragments from awareness of Essence:

- Physical experiences and pain
- Thoughts and beliefs
- Behaviour patterns
- Values
- Fantasies
- Memories: images, sound, touch, odour, taste
- sEmotions: fear, sadness, rage, anger, annoyance, terror, shame.

Different aspects of experiences we have gone through are stored in fragments like these. In them, a person's development is frozen in the moment of the incomprehensible experience. Whenever a situation similar to the moment of splitting occurs these fragments will be activated. The energy flow to the Self is interrupted. The boundaries between the person and people in the environment also are blurred.

SPLITTING EXERCISE

Concentrate on an event in the past week that disturbed, angered, or troubled you. Give yourself a few minutes to consider your answers to these questions:

- *When you recall this experience, how does it affect your thinking?*
- *What do you think about yourself, others, and the quality of life?*
- *What images and fantasies come up?*

- *What emotions come up when you remember this event?*
- *How would you rather have reacted?*
- *What reactions would you have liked from the people around you?*

- *How does the memory of this event influence your physical sensations?*
- *Where in your body do you notice this reaction?*
- *How does this place feel different from other places? Heat or cold? Mobility, stiffness, or paralysis? Strength or weakness?*

Write down your replies to the questions. Consider whether such reactions are familiar to you. It is likely that you will have reacted according to this pattern for years. This exercise may be the first steps towards freeing yourself.

INTROJECTION

When people cannot fully comprehend and process an experience, they split off elements of the consciousness of their Original Self. They store these separately, as thoughts, feelings, and sensations—splitting. This splitting process takes place within a context. A person shares his physical, social, and societal environment with other people. This context is stored along with the dissociated part. This process is called introjection—each split-off part will inevitably be connected to corresponding memories of the external world. People create representations of the outer world as they perceived it, while experiencing painful or incomprehensible experiences. These representations are very stable and contain sensory impressions of the environment at the time of the experience—what people saw, heard, smelled, tasted, and what they perceived on the surface of their bodies. The person creates a world, which is frozen in space and time. This frozen world consists of two closely connected but fundamentally different aspects:

- A representation of the environment at the time of the experience they couldn't assimilate
- An internally stored reaction to this outer world—emotional, cognitive, and physical

In terms of Logosynthesis, invisible static representations of the world are characterised as introjects or imprints. Introject means "what is thrown in" and imprint means "impression"—something from outside crosses our boundaries quickly and powerfully. Introjects are created to stabilise our perception and understanding of ourselves in the world. They are activated when something similar to the original situation occurs. Once activated, in turn, they will trigger the reactions stored in the corresponding dissociated state. Such reactions to an introject may be:

- physical,
- emotional,
- cognitive and perceptive, or
- behavioural.

Introjects are based on concrete events, in childhood or in adult life. They are installed when our previous life experience is insufficient to help us understand the outer world. Introject forms the basis of our subsequent perception and interpretation of experiences. We perceive our current environment in the light of the familiar. This may lead us to disregard aspects of the immediate present. Introjection is always connected to splitting. Introjects are stable and fulfil the need for security. Imprints of a caretaking figure provide support in their absence. Imprints of a harmful figure make the environment predictable and new experiences less alarming. Thus, splitting and introjection combine to build our frame of reference. They help people to put order on their experiences. Frozen worlds may combine to create a "complex."

The aim of Logosynthesis is to neutralise burdensome memories of people and issues. Dissociated parts and their connections to the corresponding introjects are dissolved. Deirdre's example below illustrates this point.

DEIRDRE

Deirdre was often afraid that she would get onto the wrong train. In a session with me, she examined the roots of this symptom and remembered an incident where she was trapped in a lift carrying a piano for removal. She experienced the sensation of being no longer able to breathe. Another incident happened on her first day at kindergarten when her father had brought her along and she suddenly found herself alone. In both situations, the thought "I'm lost" occurred to her. It was accompanied by feelings of fear and panic. This archaic thought triggered her current fear of getting onto the wrong train. By applying Logosynthesis, she dissolved her feelings of fear and abandonment. The introjects of the lift, the piano, and her father could be subsequently removed. As a result, her fear disappeared instantaneously. Now she consciously takes note and concentrates on where she has to go. She is more observant and aware. It helps her to stay relaxed on the train before it leaves. She doesn't have to get up to check everything. She remains calm on the journey because she knows she is well prepared.

INTROJECTS IN CHILDHOOD

The most significant imprints are formed in contact with our parents in our early childhood. They are with us for longer than anybody else, and they have the task of preparing us to find our way in society. In doing this, they impart to us their view of the world. They do this not only by what they say, but also by the way they behave towards us and others around us. We build energy constructs of our parents within our personal space and we copy and assimilate their words, attitudes, and behaviour. We do the same with others:

- Grandparents, brothers and sisters, and others who influence us

- Teachers, policemen, colleagues, and bosses
- Doctors, therapists, and counsellors
- Founders of sects and philosophies
- Individual students or entire grades in school

Slowly, we fill our personal space with imaginary statues of those around us. They come to life when we need a reference point in a new situation. Our reaction to them replicates the time when the imprints were created. Even if we may have gained insight in the meantime, rigid patterns form the basis of our reaction. When they indicate respect for ourselves and other people, we will respect ourselves in a given situation and show respect for the other person(s) also. Introjects of people who devalued or ignored us prevent us from seeing the goodwill of others.

INTROJECTS IN ADULTHOOD

Introjects are always formed if there are no other strategies available to cope with a new situation. The imprints of such events have a lasting influence on our view of ourselves, others, society, and life itself. Examples are your employer who suddenly fires you, a doctor who tells you that you have cancer, or a partner who tells you out of the blue that she's leaving home.

Sometimes a large number of people form introjects simultaneously. If you can read this book unaided then you are aware of September 11, 2001. When you're reminded of it now, you know exactly how you heard about the attacks on the Twin Towers in Manhattan. It doesn't take much to make you recall your reaction to what took place at that time. I myself remember my wife phoning me at my practice at three o'clock in the afternoon. She told me to come home and that something dreadful had happened. Five minutes later, I was sitting in front of the television watching as the Boeing 767 buried itself in the South Tower of the World Trade Centre. It literally left me breathless. We knew at that moment in time that something fundamental had changed in the world, even though we couldn't appreciate its historical significance.

Older readers will recall the assassination of John F. Kennedy on November 22, 1963 in a similar fashion. He was unable to fulfil his promise of a better world. The optimism of the Kennedy years vanished with that shooting in Dallas, Texas.

INTROJECTS AS FRAGMENTS OF PERCEPTION

Introjects do not need to represent an entire person. A particular sensory experience may contribute to the formation of a frozen world. It might be the loud voice of a primary-school teacher, the contorted face of a furious mother, or the hand that strikes a child when he wasn't even expecting it. Breaking the physical boundaries in instances of sexual abuse leaves extremely strong introjects. Single sentences can also be deeply inscribed in our experience of the world. I vividly remember the prophetic words of my Spanish golf pro, "You'll never learn this sport." Others imply that we have certain characteristics, such as, "I've never met anyone as stupid as you." Then there are those that identify us with other people, saying, "You're just like Aunt Martha." If Aunt Martha is clever, this will be reassuring, but if she's a sick alcoholic, this message may lead to misery.

INTROJECTS ARE NOT LIMITED TO PEOPLE

Not only people leave traces in our energy system. Other sensory impressions, as well as their rational and irrational processing, may establish themselves as energy structures. These may be located within or on our body, or in our personal space. All introjects can generate a conditioned emotional reaction that can restrict our freedom. Some examples are places where people have lived or worked, for example:

- houses or rooms—bathroom, kitchen, basement;
- landscapes, trees, streets, fountains; and
- buildings—schools, churches, hospitals, prisons.

Introjects are also formed when children are suddenly abandoned by their parents and only strangers are there to take care of them. The first thing that they perceive is the physical environment without their parents, as in Deirdre's case on page 18. Institutions and their rules can also install strong introjects, for example:

- churches, workplaces, political parties, employers;
- abstract concepts—guilt, wrongful actions, marriage, divorce, communism, democracy;
- values—freedom, progress;
- country—your own country, neighbouring countries, world powers; and
- media messages—television, newspapers, advertising, the internet.

A few years ago, I wanted to find a quiet retreat to work on a book. I chose a hundred-year-old spa hotel in Tessin, the sunniest spot in Switzerland. This turned out to be extremely unfortunate. The architecture of the building was almost identical to the pulmonary rehabilitation centre in Davos where I had worked for many years. I was confronted by my previous workplace in every corner of the hotel. It took me a lot of time and effort to neutralise this vivid picture and concentrate on the piece of work I intended.

INTROJECTS ON THE BODY

Physical objects can also cause introjects. The piano in the lift in Deirdre's experience is one example. It led to constricted breathing, which in turn raised her anxiety on the train. In my book *Logosynthesis – Change through the Magic of Words*, I described the case of Fred who had fallen out of a tree as a child. As a result, he suffered from a fear that took away from his enjoyment of climbing. He had fallen on the root of a tree and had broken his arm. In the treatment session, a representation of this root emerged in his body. It led to a physical tension and triggered the anxiety reaction.

In a similar case, a seminar participant had been struck by the bumper of a car. Since then, he had suffered from chronic pain in his right leg. During the seminar, he had already freed himself from the emotional effects of the accident. However, the pain remained, and an energetic imprint of the bumper of the car in his leg with it. In subsequent treatment, he retrieved his own energy, which had been bound up in the image of the bumper, and remove its energy from his system. Afterwards, the pain disappeared instantaneously and never returned (see also page 61).

INTROJECTS OF PLACES

Lydia provided an example of how place can also form introjects. She was taking part in a Logosynthesis group and had difficulty finding her way with the other participants. In exploring this problem, it emerged that as a child she had lived on the side of a wide road. Crossing the road had been very dangerous because of the heavy traffic. Her parents were very concerned that something would happen to their only child. All her friends lived the other side of the road. This left her sad and lonely. This childhood sadness was reactivated in the group. She felt excluded and experienced herself once again on the other side of the road. By means of Logosynthesis, she managed to dissolve the imprint of the wide road and begin to communicate with the group.

THE MEDIA, ADVERTISING, THE INTERNET

The media provides plenty of introjects. We can only comprehend quite a small portion of the world through our immediate sensory experiences. The media communicate the rest to us. That's why they are called "the media." Advertising plays a special part in the process. It tries to establish new introjects that will be activated when we go shopping. People prefer to buy a familiar brand to a new one. The attractive images used in television advertising lead us to believe that we will be equally happy if we buy the product being promoted. When advertising focuses on new concepts like irritable bowel syndrome or sensitive skin, we're inclined to examine our bodies for the newly-discovered symptom. We consult the internet to find out the rest. Since we do this in a state of uncertainty, there is a good chance that we'll introject the information without making any evaluation. Eventually, our doctor will have to deal with the resulting myths about health and remedies.

FROZEN WORLDS

Unprocessed, traumatic events are split off from the consciousness of the Original Self and stored along with a representation of the environment. The dissociated part, together with an introject, forms a rigid, unchanging world, frozen in space and time—a time capsule. In this capsule, the energy flow to and from the Original Self is impeded or blocked. The time capsule impedes the flow of energy between the Original Self and the environment. Our boundaries in space and time become unclear. We really don't know who we are or where we are—one part of us exists in the past and another part is trying to find a meaning in the here-and-now. The frozen world filters our perception of the here-and-now and causes us to relive traumatic experiences. We tend to react exactly as we did when we were unable to understand the world around us.

INTROJECTION EXERCISE

Look back at the memories from the exercise on page 17. What exactly are the internal representations of the event that trigger your emotional and physical reaction?

- *What do you see at the various stages of the incident? People, objects, locations?*
- *What do you hear that provokes a reaction? Voices, music, noise?*

- *What do you sense on your skin? Heat, coldness, vibration, a current?*
- *What do you smell?*

The frozen world is a combination of the recollection of the external world and your physical, emotional, and mental reactions at the time of the incident. If you've experienced a major fire in your own house, you will immediately activate that frozen world whenever you smell smoke. Your reactions to the actual situation will be guided by the earlier experience. By applying Logosynthesis, you can learn to identify and resolve such frozen worlds. You will free the energy bound up in the event for the fulfilment of you individual life's purpose. Energy will flow freely to and from Essence.

THE SELF

The living adult Self comprises what remains of the Original Self following much splitting. It governs the dynamic life experience formed by successfully processed information, events, and incidents. The Self is open to any occasion to develop itself or others. It also has the capacity to enclose itself in the here-and-now when danger is imminent. The Self is aware of the boundaries between itself and others.

ARE YOU YOUR OWN BOSS?

Many of us lack awareness of Essence in everyday life. We don't recognise our mission and allow ourselves to be distracted and led by our physical selves, the ambition of our ego and our environment. This gets to the point where we lose all control over our own lives. Many counsellors give tips telling us what we should do—how to think positive, live out our dreams, successfully overcome conflicts, manage our time, let our creativity sparkle, and have the courage to be proactive. Why does this not work? In the book it's all very easy, and when the expert explains the ideas, they're easily understood, but splitting and introjection prevent the transfer of what we read. We let ourselves be driven from one demand to another in the bus of everyday life instead of taking the wheel ourselves. When we are living out of Essence, we don't need any book to manage our time and carry out our plans.

Research on cognition uses the term "executive" to describe our internal mental executive function. You will already be familiar with the term in a different context: the CEO is the *chairperson of the executive office*, in contrast with the board of directors who devise the strategy. Are you powerful enough to take that office in accordance with Essence? Or, alternatively, do you jump from the outside world to an introject and from the introject to a dissociated state, from each on to the next?

Most people lack power in their daily lives. Initially they are dominated by parents. When parents fade into the background or die, their statues occupy their personal space. To the left is the father with the mother in front or the other way round. They are unable to tell the difference between the others in their world and these images. The boss is transformed into the father figure and the female colleague into the mother figure. Is this true for you? Try the following brief exercise:

Put two blank sheets of paper on a table one on top of the other. Then think of someone that you're finding it hard to get on with, a "difficult" person—a friend, a colleague, or your boss. Imagine this person on the top sheet. The paper will remain blank but let your inner eye draw the picture…

As soon as this picture has become clear, move on to the next step. Pick someone from your personal history of whom the "difficult" person reminds you. Visualise this second picture over the image of the first person on the blank sheet.

Now separate the two images. To do this, you slowly move the two sheets apart. The image of the "difficult" person remains on the top sheet. The image of the second will move to the bottom sheet.
Separate the pictures completely and let your eyes focus on the sheet that was on the bottom before. Study your reaction to the picture of the person from your past.

Finally change your focus to the other sheet and examine your reaction to the "difficult" person in your life at present. What has changed?

After this exercise, most people report that they can react to the person in their present more calmly and less negative. They separate the actual person from the earlier frozen introject. They notice that they can now choose their reaction. The power to act lies in their own hands. The introjects no longer correspond to the real world. The earlier reaction and dissociated state will not be triggered either.

2.3.
Axiom 3. Energy in Space

"A monk asked the abbot, Rufos: 'What is peace of heart and what are its benefits?'
The old man said: 'Peace of heart means sitting (in the hermitage) with reverence to find God. It means transcending the recollection of suffering and pride. Such peace is the mother of all virtue.'

– EVARGIUS, IN DANIEL HELL (2007)

THE THIRD KEY AXIOM

Dissociated parts and introjects are energy constructs frozen in three-dimensional space.

PERSONAL SPACE EXERCISE

The following exercise will help you learn more about personal space so you can understand our third axiom more easily. Find an area of at least twelve to fifteen square metres where you can move around easily. Walk slowly a few times round this area. Then find a spot in the centre where you have room to move in any direction. Now observe yourself within this space.

- *What emotions are you experiencing at this moment?*
- *How does your body feel?*
- *Is it relaxed or tense?*
- *Where is the tension?*
- *How is your breathing? Deep or shallow? Fast or slow?*

Locate the boundaries of your personal space. Where does this space now begin when other people enter? Where do you perceive the boundaries of your space?

- *In front of you? Behind you?*
- *To your left or right?*
- *Above you? Below you?*
- *How is your personal space different from the outer world? Does it feel warmer? Colder? More dense? Does it seem brighter, darker, or more colourful? Does it have different vibrations from the world outside?*

Next, imagine different people within your personal space. As a start, choose one significant other in your life like your mother, father, partner, child, friend, or boss. Examine how they influence the experience of your personal space.

- *Exactly where in space does this person's image appear? In front of you, behind you, to your right, or to your left? Above you or below you?*
- *How far from you is their image?*
- *What is your internal reaction to the person's image in space? Watch out for emotions like fear, anger, pain,*

shame, dislike, or joy. Note also physical sensations such as heat, cold, pressure, or pain.

- *Does the rhythm of your breathing change when you focus on this image in your personal space? Faster or slower? Deeper or shallower?*
- *Do your physical sensations then change as a reaction to the person's image?*
- *Imagine the image completely disappearing from your personal space. Now how do you change your reactions?*

Next repeat this exercise for two more significant others one after the other.

ENERGY BLOCKS

In Logosynthesis, dissociated parts and introjects are more than just metaphors or abstract psychological concepts. They are energetic realities. We construct them using our own Life Energy inside or outside our bodies, within our personal space or outside of it. We ourselves don't form them completely. Others also can add their own energy to your introjects. If we free our personal space of such constructs, the peace of heart of the abbot from the quotation above will enter our lives. Our personal space in the solitude of our personal hermitage is filled with memories and fantasies that interrupt the flow of our Life Energy in the here-and-now. It's no wonder that people have also retired from the busy world to reconnect to Essence—a hermitage provides the ideal environment to examine frozen worlds.

Einstein previously noticed the connection between matter and energy even though he probably didn't think of such an application of his theory. Parts of our Life Energy may be in other places than where it belongs. The parts are split off at the time of traumatic experiences and stay in other places within our body or in space. Dissociated parts may overflow into the space occupied by the body. They may also be further away, as you can see from the example of Erik.

ERIK

Erik, a former top volleyball player, had broken the little finger of his left hand several times on the playing field. The finger became stiff and immobile after these injuries. After having an artificial joint implanted it was still extremely painful when he moved it, even several weeks later. During his work with Logosynthesis, it became obvious that an energy fragment of the finger was behind his back at shoulder level. The part was split off and frozen there when the volleyball unfortunately struck his little finger in the excitement of the match. Using Logosynthesis, Erik took back the displaced energy to where it belonged, in his physical finger. The pain disappeared immediately. He could start to move the joint, and a few weeks later the joint was fully functional without any pain.

LEONORE

The example of Leonore shows that not only dissociated states but also introjects have three-dimensional components. During our session, Leonore told me how she was afraid of the approaching medical examination of her cervical vertebrae, which had been injured in an accident. Her fear was triggered by the memory of a professor who had treated her rudely, in fact roughly, during an earlier examination. When Leonore described her fear of a further meeting with the professor, she was continuously moving her head to the right. It seemed as if somebody on her left kept talking to her loudly and she was trying to escape. When I asked her where in the room the professor's image was located Leonore gestured towards her left ear and described how the professor yelled at her from about thirty centimetres away.

In Leonore's perception, the professor was really in the room and her body actually reacted to this presence. When I asked her to remove the professor's image from her personal space, her fear of the next examination immediately disappeared. It subsequently went smoothly.

THE BODY REACTS TO INTROJECTS

Not merely parts of a person's ego-consciousness may be displaced; introjects of significant others and aspects of the environment also can be located within our body or in our personal space. Such representations affect those concerned as if they were real people in the same space. The body also tends to react as if the person represented were actually present. If we accept that the professor really exists as an energy construct within Leonore's personal space and that his presence is detrimental to the her well-being, it's good to remove it. When the professor's image disappeared, the fear of a future meeting with one of his colleagues was resolved. This provided the foundation for two important working hypotheses:

1. We don't always experience ourselves in the same place as our physical body in three-dimensional space. We may be fragmented.
2. Our body, as well as the three-dimensional space surrounding us, contains representations of other people and objects. As soon as these representations cross certain physical boundaries, they directly affect our thoughts, feelings, and emotions. Our personal space is the space within these boundaries. Introjects affect us deeply when our physical boundaries have been violently penetrated.

IRMA

Irma told me during a session how she had designed an exercise for herself. She would lay down a rope in the shape of a circle around her—she defined this circle as her personal space. Irma described how initially she had laid the rope quite close to herself. Then she experimented to see how big she could make the circle before it became uncomfortable. She noticed she was able to relax more and more as she learnt to increase her personal space in the course of psychotherapy.

OUR BOUNDARIES ARE THREE-DIMENSIONAL

Irma's experiment illustrated that we perceive part of the space surrounding us as our own. When an object or thought form occupies this space, it will provoke a more powerful reaction than outside of this personal space. Introjects also can enter the space occupied by our bodies, they may be in the immediate proximity of our body, or be located beyond it. In the latter case, they trigger almost no physical or archaic reaction. The monk frees the personal space of his hermitage from the shadows of the past, his wishes, and his fantasies. Cleaning his personal space opens his consciousness to the full force of a greater power.

SELF-COACHING THROUGH LOGOSYNTHESIS

The application of Logosynthesis can dissolve the frozen energy traces of the past and establish your own boundaries in space. Using the sentences you will retrieve your personal energy from the frozen world and direct it back to yourself. You will remove the remaining traces of frozen worlds from your body and personal space. You will, thus, activate the power of your creative intention. Consequently, you will recognise your life task without difficulty. The Self will take control.

2.4.
Axiom 4. Words Create

"A song is sleeping in all things
It's dreaming on and on
And the world will start to sing
Once you hit the magic word."

– JOSEF VON EICHENDORFF

THE FOURTH KEY AXIOM

Words and sentences have an active creative power beyond their inherent content and emotional significance.

THE WORD AS CREATOR

The fourth axiom of Logosynthesis is the least widely understood. Many people show resistance in recognising and accepting it as an independent principle. Our usual thinking is deeply embedded in words. It is a novel and unimaginable idea that words can have the power to create—a power which is in fact disrupted by thoughts. This is the greatest difference between Logosynthesis and other methods of personal change and spiritual development. The power of

Logosynthesis is directly founded on the creative power of the Word, without any conscious mental effort.

Since the Enlightenment, Western culture has ignored, even repressed, the concept of a creative power of the Word. Before, it was a widespread element of culture. René Descartes differentiated between a *res extensa* and a *res cogitans*, what we would call body and mind. The third aspect of human existence, called Essence in this book, fell by the wayside in a new, pragmatic view of the world. Descartes' statement *cogito ergo sum*—I think therefore I am—equally identifies the thinker's existence with his capacity to process information. The software becomes the user. This reduction allowed for the study of many different types of patterns in nature and Man. The sciences founded on this basis consequently reduced Essence to patterns in matter and energy.

From the beginning of recorded human history and the start of our own lives, words have been a means to describe our world, to form concepts, to construct theories and to broaden our life experience. There is, however, another view of the word—as a creative principle *in itself*. This perspective is not based on linguistics, psychology, or philosophy, which are based on rationalism and reductionism, following Descartes and his successors. The Word as a manifestation of creative intention can only be discovered through an alternative avenue.

Etymology and spiritual traditions see many connections between words and intention, creativity, development, and change. The Word has a meaning and power beyond all human understanding. In this tradition, even the world has its origin in words. They have an unfathomable creative potential. Words manifesting intention constitute the quintessence of the act of creation. In the first verse of St. John's Gospel, the word is directly associated with God:

"In the beginning was the Word
and the Word was with God
and the Word was God."

Words have the intrinsic quality to focus and manifest the speaker's creative intention. The intended appears if the right words are said, without any effort or rational achievement from the speaker. God's word has an immediate effect on the physical world; it even creates it. The Word is also the quintessence of creation in other early writings. The Old Testament, Genesis 1:3 states:

"And God spoke:
'Let there be light,' and there was light."

The Koran is also explicit in this sense (6:73):

"If Allah decides something, He simply says:
'Let there be'—and there is."

In religious and spiritual writings, the Word per se is able to activate creative energy, *without rational information processing*. The creative power of the Word is founded on a separate teleological originating principle, which is fundamentally different from the law of cause and effect that is dominant in our current thinking, and, therefore, is difficult to grasp. This principle was familiar in the Middle Ages, but has been more or less ignored since the Age of Enlightenment. Our culture has a high regard for the principle of cause and effect based on three-dimensional, material, quantifiable entities. In physics, it is becoming increasingly evident, in that reality is not as simply constructed as Newton, Galilei, and Copernicus has lead us to believe. Nevertheless, many models of the human psyche advance a single theory that reflects the frame of reference of physics in the stage of the steam engine.

WORDS AND ETYMOLOGICAL EVOLUTION

Etymology studies the roots of our language. It reveals interesting connections between the linguistic form of a word and its evolution. Hence, our expression *Word*, the German *Wort* (word) and *werden* (to become) are quite close. The Dutch even have retained the o—they speak of *woord* and *worden.* The same applies to *sagen* (to say) and *Segen* (blessing)—in dutch, *zeggen* and *zegen.* The Dutch use the same word to mean "sentence" and "meaning": *zin.* In Greek, the words *arche* (beginning) and *logos* (word, speech, meaning) have the same etymological roots. Linguistic experts can continue such correspondences indefinitely.

THE WORD IN HUMANS

The manifesting, "magical" power of the Word also has a tradition in human history. It endures despite being considered non-scientific and irrational:

- For thousands of years, people have prayed to have their wishes granted or to achieve their goals. New research seems to confirm these effects. Concepts like suggestion and placebo effect are not really providing solid explanations for this, and it seems that a paradigm shift is needed.

- Curses and blessings are attempts to bring those close to us into good or bad circumstances.
- In many small communities, there still are women who have the power to "put a spell on" warts to make them disappear.
- Certain Middle Eastern cultures have single words that when said aloud will lame a scorpion instantly.
- Hypnotism, suggestion, and autogenic training directly affect our physical functions
- Every child knows there is only one real magic spell: *Abrakadabra.* This incantation comes from the Aramaic *avrah ka dabra*, which supports our argument: *I am creating while I speak.*

THE WORD IN LOGOSYNTHESIS

In Logosynthesis, the creative, manifesting power of the Word is directly employed as a tool for change to re-integrate fragmented consciousness and dissolve frozen introjects. Certain precisely formed sentences have a unique definitive power. This power is far greater than its usual meaning, which makes Logosynthesis a unique means of personal and spiritual development.

3.
Method

Logosynthesis is a technique for guided change and for self-coaching, better described as a method of being coached by yourself. Your Self, the manifested Essence, is the best coach there is. Why?

- It always has a well-defined goal in view.
- It will pursue this goal courageously and unrelentingly.
- It communicates closely with others and respects their potential and their limitations.
- It similarly respects its own abilities and limitations and can, therefore, establish appropriate priorities.
- It can decide which talents it needs to utilise at any given moment.
- It can draw on its entire store of knowledge at all times.
- Its emotions operate as an early warning system for risks and opportunities.
- It acknowledges when it needs help itself. It is not alone, nor does it become dependent.
- It is ready to learn.

In today's business world, you couldn't buy a coach like this. Yet you already have him. This coach is by your side, always. Logosynthesis will help you to discover this coach and have him walk with you. The process will not be completed overnight. You may have not listened to him for years and possibly can no longer hear him.

When you begin to apply Logosynthesis to issues in your own life, I advise you to take small steps. If you want too much at once, you run the risk that the effect will fizzle out. You may then lose the motivation to continue. It is easy to find out whether you are trying to go too quickly. If applying Logosynthesis causes impatience, anger, irritation, or sadness, you should reduce the tempo and deal with these issues alone. Realise how long you have run the patterns that now rule your life. Take the time to gain a gradual and thorough understanding of the techniques so you can apply them to issues that are more important. Initially, not much of your Self's consciousness is at your disposal. To deal with more significant issues, you will need more. The more energy, information, and consciousness of Essence are flowing, the easier Essence will resolve new issues. For many people, Logosynthesis has become part of everyday life. Their tolerance for negative patterns is significantly reduced—they work with them as soon as they notice them. The best method of overcoming initial impatience is to apply it to many minor issues systematically. You will learn when and exactly how it takes effect for you. You will learn to detect and appreciate the minor changes. You will need this skill to work on larger issues that have been there for most of your life. After a while, you will find that each time you apply Logosynthesis, the effect will be different. It will range between huge relief concerning your entire body and all your emotions, and a slight relaxation of your forehead muscles.

The self-application of Logosynthesis involves six aspects:

1. The basic attitude
2. Focusing
3. Saying the sentences
4. Letting go
5. New cycles
6. The transfer

You can't omit or short-circuit any of the following points:

- The basic attitude is essential to set the process in motion.
- Focusing will help you to cut the salami of your life issues into digestible pieces.
- The sentences will initiate the process of change.
- Let go of rational control for the fragments to reintegrate and imprints to dissolve.
- Work with next issues that show up.
- Return to daily life and consciously notice the change.

3.1.
The Basic Attitude

The basic attitude in any application of Logosynthesis can be explained in two words: curiosity and patience. You don't consciously act, guide, or control apart from the steps described in this chapter. Your ego doesn't need to achieve. In our culture, we're accustomed to actively defining and creating our own happiness. In Logosynthesis, you don't need to; your Self knows. If you're not happy, dissociative influences keep you from becoming happy, and your Self knows how to dissolve them. Logosynthesis offers a way to let your Self take control of your life. That makes it a great deal easier to define your personal happiness:

- You learn what you really want.
- You recognise and take advantage of opportunities to progress on your path.
- You have a positive open communication with other people and less interpersonal conflict.
- You're capable of supporting others when it's needed.
- You're able to get help whenever you need it.

The application of Logosynthesis is founded on the basic principle that our own Self knows what's important. This is why it's important to enlarge awareness of the Self rather than let yourself be influenced by temporarily activated introjects or current dissociative influences. By its nature, dissociation will obstruct our path when:

- we like to be in control of our life at all times;
- we prefer to tackle a problem the way we believe in, irrespective of other ways;
- we avoid unpleasant emotions and conditions; or
- we're impatient.

The goal of Logosynthesis is to activate a continuous conscious access to your Self. This will solve your problems and support your personal and spiritual development. It will be a more effective and efficient process if you stick to a few simple rules, especially at the beginning. In time, you'll follow the rules automatically. They are the rules of the Self:

- Take your time.
- Work in small steps.
- Try it on everything!
- Keep going!

In Logosynthesis, small issues will only take up a few minutes while more significant ones will demand a few hours. Major issues may take a few days. Don't be surprised if it takes years to process the issues you've been carrying all your life.

You will need to be very aware of Essence to tackle the bigger issues. You'll find this is true as you tackle more and more minor issues. The big advantage with Logosynthesis is that you'll get a feeling of achievement right from the start. It will reassure that you're going in the right direction.

Many of us are unaware that beneath the surface of everyday existence so many issues lie unresolved, and new ones arise from day to day. The Self is smart—as soon as it finds a strategy to deal with unresolved issues it will immediately bring new fragments to the surface; it has a stake in your development. Logosynthesis will accelerate this process, as soon as you start to accept that all your emotions linked to the past are basically redundant energy structures and can be dissolved. To get to this point, however, it's essential to experience that after the dissolution of the earlier, frozen world, a new world will show up, literally "by itself" or more exactly: "by your Self." This new world promises many more opportunities than the old, dissociated one. The longing for the old familiar feelings will diminish with training in the application of Logosynthesis. It will bring openness and curiosity concerning the present. In the early years following the discovery of Logosynthesis, I spent hours each day dissolving dissociated states and introjects. In the course of time, the process advanced more quickly as more and more energy, information, and consciousness of the Self became available for day-to-day living. This made it easier to identify split-off parts and introjects, and apply Logosynthesis to them. Initially it may be challenging that a seemingly minor issue turns out to be a very complicated major one. If this is the case, you need to learn how to focus the application of the technique specifically. As you progress, your Self will naturally take control. You'll find it easier all the time to identify and dissolve parts and introjects that belong in the past.

3.2.
Focusing

THE CURRENT STATE

Before you begin the practical application of Logosynthesis, choose an issue to work on. You will have an infinite choice. Start with issues that don't feel too big, that you can observe and understand well. Your answers to the questions below can provide material for Logosynthesis:

- *What are your aims and dreams in life—in your relationships, work, personal development, and material concerns? If you're failing to realise each one, what's holding you back?*
- *How do you react to this failure—in your body, thoughts, beliefs, emotions, and behaviour patterns?*
- *What are the important relationships in your life? Which of these are problematic?*
- *How do you react to these relationships—in your body, thoughts, beliefs, emotions, and behaviour patterns?*

FOCUSING ON EMOTIONAL STATES

Examine your thoughts and feelings related to these issues and record them in a journal. The list below will help you to identify your emotional states more accurately:

- Frustration
- Disappointment
- Anger/fury/defiance/aggression
- Mistrust

- Fear/uncertainty
- Having an adequate or excessive amount of something
- Aversion/reluctance
- Concern/worry
- Lack of enthusiasm/low mood
- Restlessness/impatience/uneasiness
- Sadness/longing
- Helplessness
- Contempt
- Envy/jealousy/gloating

Many difficult situations are associated with a combination of the states listed above. If Logosynthesis does not prove immediately effective, it is worth considering which emotions have become less intense and which are predominant.

FOCUSING ON PHYSICAL SIGNS

Physical signs and symptoms are also a good means of familiarising yourself with Logosynthesis. We have an immediate physical reaction when something is the matter. Many of us can see it by the range of symptoms usually associated with stress. Here are a few examples:

- Tiredness, exhaustion
- Muscular tension
- Uneasiness within yourself
- Trembling
- Racing heart
- Sweating

- Stomach-ache
- A feeling of fullness
- Craving for food, drinks, nicotine
- And so on

Each of these symptoms is linked to a high level of emotional distress. They're upsetting, even if you might not consult a doctor about them. Yet they make a good starting point for applying Logosynthesis. You can usually define a stressor fairly accurately by the relevant symptom. This means you must be watchful for any slight changes.

THE SUD SCALE

The Scale to measure Subjective Units of Distress (SUDs) is useful in assessing your present situation and becoming aware of the changes that using Logosynthesis will bring. Concentrate on one single aspect of the problems in the list above and ask yourself:

How uncomfortable is this problem on a scale from zero to ten?

A score of zero means that the issue is not at all stressful. A zero means you have no difficulty remaining calm and composed. You have a whole range of options to choose from in overcoming challenges in your life. It's different with a ten; here the distress is so high that you no longer see a way round the problem. Any given problem can be rated between one and ten on the scale. If you're bad at figures, use a smiley-scale, with a sad smiley on the left and a smiling one on the right.

THE DESIRED STATE

Many schools of self-development consider it important that you define your own goals. Thereby, they often ignore that truly meaningful goals can only be formulated only in contact with Essence. If your connection to Essence is weak, your goals will inevitably be influenced by the interests of the ego. That means that they will hardly be appropriate in helping you on your most profound personal journey. Split parts and introjects will continuously prevent you from finding the true significance of your thoughts, feelings, and life circumstances. It, therefore, is of little use to invent all too vivid images of the future if fragments of your consciousness and introjects from the past distort your awareness in the here-and-now. In Logosynthesis, it's enough to know that the Self will know where the path is leading, as soon as you've released the obstacles from the past. You won't need to coach the Self. Let it coach you. The Self has no interest in suffering. It will confront issues and cooperate instantly when it can see a way out of the pain. Your path is a winding, hilly one into the unknown. Using Logosynthesis will help you to see around the next turn or over the next mountain. When you gain this overview, it will be much easier to find and explore new goals that Essence brings to your life.

FOCUSING: A VISIT FROM YOUR MOTHER-IN-LAW

You start with identifying the issue you want to work on through Logosynthesis. The next step is to choose a single aspect of that issue. At the beginning, it is especially important to select well-defined, easily managed issues. Why?

- You should gradually increase the influence of the Self in your life. The easiest way to achieve this is by working on a number of minor issues.
- It's a good idea to confront more significant issues through Logosynthesis only when you're experienced in the use of the technique. Once the Self has taken a certain influence in your life, it will show you new options and will expand its range.

As an example, we will now apply focusing strategies on the occasion if a visit from your mother-in-law on a holiday or birthday celebration. Your career doesn't depend on it, but if you don't deal with the situation properly, it'll escalate. Begin with the following situation: your mother-in-law has been invited. You too agreed to invite her, but the prospect of her coming to dinner is enough to spoil your birthday celebration.

It's important not to tackle the entire issue at once in applying Logosynthesis to the situation. You should deal with the situation that's getting you down. On the one hand, you have introjects. These are the energetic representations of your mother-in-law in your personal space, such as:

- your most recent telephone conversation when she wasn't really friendly to you;
- her shrill voice when she tells a story at the table;
- her face when she's read the riot act to your children; or
- the faces of your family members when the situation got out of hand.

Notice where the image of your mother-in-law is located in your personal space, or even in your body. This will help you analyse any changes. The other side of this difficult situation is your own consistent, less-than-perfect reaction, which is a dissociated state:

- You feel annoyed at the thought that your mother-in-law is coming over.
- You're ashamed that things have gone so far that you're upset by her visit.
- You feel guilty for thinking about a lonely, old woman in such terms.
- Your heart races when you visualise your mother-in law at your celebration dinner.

Now choose an aspect from the list and rate your distress on a scale of zero to ten. Apply the technique to the chosen aspect. When you've neutralised it, move on to the next aspect. Given time and experience, you'll get an indication of all that you can achieve using Logosynthesis. Remember, it won't all happen at once.

3.3.
Saying the Sentences

"My life is proceeding effortlessly
I don't even feel the previous blocks."

– A CLIENT

SANDRA MAKES MUSIC

Sandra gets stage fright when she has to play the piano in front of audiences. She says:

"I watch myself playing the piano and I go all tense."

So she's dissociated—she has a playing and a watching part. The playing part is in contact with the fear and the bodily tension. She is given a sentence to repeat:

I retrieve all my energy bound up in the fear of playing the piano in public and take it back to the right place within my Self.

Sandra:

"I become a bit calmer."

The energy of the fear has returned to the Self. Then she is given another sentence:

I retrieve all my energy bound up in the person watching me play the piano and take it back to the right place within my Self.

Sandra:

"I start feeling sad and can't play anymore."

Another dissociated part now shows up, in which she's sad. The critical introject probably becomes more active. Then she receives a third sentence:

I remove the rest of the energy of the person watching me play the piano from my personal space and send it out into the Light.

Sandra repeats the sentence, and there is a long, deep silence. Then she says:

"I'm playing music, not notes!"

The introject is removed, and the Self has taken over. It's always the Self that makes the real music.

THE EFFECT OF THE SENTENCES

What is Sandra doing? Surprisingly, little. She is repeating sentences. When she pauses after the sentences, these deploy their healing power. Her frozen worlds dissolve and she re-establishes contact with Essence. She doesn't need to do. She doesn't need to think. There is no effort. She doesn't visualise goals. She doesn't even need to believe. It's enough if she repeats the sentences, lets them take effect and observe how they do so. Especially at the beginning of the process, this is difficult to understand or even imagine. It borders on magic and casting spells. You may be doubtful and ask yourself, *"If it's all so simple, what have I been doing wrong up to now?"* You've done nothing wrong, and your life experience stays just as valid if you work with Logosynthesis. However, you may give up some beliefs that you now hold strongly; there are other ways to change. Change doesn't always need reliving the pain of the past. It doesn't always need interpretation or reflection. In my life, I studied many ways to bring about change in people, and I've put a lot of time and energy in learning to guide the development of people. Many schools of change deliver great insight but their models and methods contribute too little to reducing actual human suffering.

Since the founding of Logosynthesis, scepticism has been my faithful companion, in long inner dialogues, and in my encounters with other experts. Strange enough, my clients were the least sceptical. Sceptics will try to reduce the power of the Word to well-known concepts. Empty psychological clichés such as "affirmation," "trance," "suggestion." or "placebo effect" cannot define this unique effect. If you're sceptical, set aside your arguments against Logosynthesis, just for an hour and take the simple steps involved for a small issue of your choice. Then you will learn how the power of the Word takes effect without any effort of your mind. It will bring a new peaceful dimension to your self-awareness.

If you appreciate that, you can do your Self another favour and remove the energy of those sceptical imprints from your energy system.

THE PROCEDURE

Applying Logosynthesis involves a clearly defined series of interventions concerning a wide range of issues. Before you apply it, you should focus on a single issue and examine the current state. Then you'll gain experience and monitor the process as it advances. When you have identified the problem and focused on it, there are two different interventions, with two different types of sentences, you can try. You'll understand them clearly after having read the chapter on dissociation. The interventions are:

1. retrieval and
2. removal.

These interventions are repeated individually, or in combination, until change or relief takes place. In both steps, you follow the same procedure when you have focused:

- Finding the Logosynthesis sentence
- Saying the sentence
- Pausing to let the sentence sink in, relaxing, and observing your internal process
- Transitioning to a new state with its corresponding relaxation and relief

This process is different to any previous techniques for change. This applies even when the individual aspects of the process have a certain similarity to other models of personal and spiritual change and development. It's usual to focus on an issue. The process of change may also be initiated by other methods. In talking therapies, the client is invited to reflect on his feelings or analyse the emotions connected to his thoughts. With EMDR (Eye Movement Desensitisation and Reprocessing by Francine Shapiro), the client brings a stressful situation to mind while following the therapist's finger-movements with his eyes. Energy Psychology techniques such as EFT (Emotional Freedom Technique by Gary Craig) and TFT (Thought Field Therapy by Roger Callahan) require that certain acupuncture points are stimulated in a prescribed sequence while the client concentrates on an issue. With Logosynthesis, clearly defined sentences are repeated. This will provide a similar or even more profound effect. Most techniques for guided change need a trained professional to apply them. In Logosynthesis, you can start to change your thoughts, beliefs, emotions, and behaviour without the help of a professional, if you carefully follow the directions further on in this chapter. However, as in any developmental process, it might make sense to get support if archaic emotions become too intensive for you to direct the change process. In that case, you can ask a friend or your partner who has also read the book and who can guide you through the steps. In the appendix, you will find information about professionals who can support you. If you're a trained professional in coaching, counselling, or psychotherapy, you'll also find details on further training in Logosynthesis.

THE START-UP PHASE

The start-up phase brings you in contact with your Self and will involve it in the change process. Take a few minutes to relax and then say the sentence:

I activate my Essence for my development throughout this process.

For "Essence," you may use "true Self," "higher Self," "real Self," or a term that suits you. Repeat this sentence several times. If you believe in God, you can pray for Him to assist you in your application of Logosynthesis for your development. Then allow a calm, relaxed interval of up to one minute, and let the sentence sink in. At the same time, note your sense perceptions, physical sensations, and beginnings of internal dialogue and emotion.

At this stage, it is most important to possess an inner openness to the healing energy of the word and the true Self. Shut out anything that distracts you from the process. When you have repeated the sentences, observe your thoughts and feelings as if they were the proverbial passing white clouds in a blue sky. The effect of this step is usually a first relief. At this point, you're able activate your true Self at the beginning of a Logosynthesis application. In time, this step will become unnecessary.

Work at your own pace; don't try to speed up that process. For new aspects, emotions, observations, beliefs, and symptoms, it's frequently repeated. Initially, the tempo will seem very slow. That's because your mind doesn't have anything to do when the words are working. When the application is running, it does so *by itself* in the truest sense of the word. For positive advancement in the use of Logosynthesis, you need that underlying attitude of patience and curiosity that dictates you to slow down, to let go and to let things happen.

SENTENCE 1. RETRIEVING ONE'S OWN ENERGY

After preparing and focusing on your issue, you should take some time to allow the initial sentence to sink in. In the first sentence, the Self removes its energy bound up in frozen past worlds and restores it to the right place in itself.

THE SENTENCE

Sentence 1, also termed the "retrieval sentence," reads as follows:

I retrieve all the energy bound up in (event, person, place) X and take it back to the right place in my Self.

At first, it's useful to write down the sentence before repeating it, especially if it consists of more than seven words. This is not a memory exercise. The power of the Word will do all the work. It involves no sorrow, emotion, stress, demands, or thought. Nor is there any need to wave your arms about, breathe deeply, or maintain a set physical posture. You just repeat the sentence.

THE PAUSE IN THE PROCESS

What happens next is truly amazing—the effect of the power of the Word. When you have repeated the sentence, you let go. You surrender to the process and observe curiously how the sentence works. There's no need to try anything with your mind. Let go, relax, and monitor your body—breathing, pulse, overall mood, emotions, and thoughts. Be also aware of changes in your perception of your surroundings. The air may feel fresher, your vision may become clearer or more colourful, or the room may become more silent.

Allow enough time for the pause, especially in the beginning of your work with Logosynthesis. This is similar to the gardener who allows his flowers to grow in their own right or the concert-goer enjoying the music. Let it happen the way you would indulge in a massage.

It's a good idea to repeat the sentence and the corresponding pause, especially the first time, or if you have little experience yet. In any case, repeat the sentence during the pause in the process:

- if you find yourself losing concentration,
- if intensive emotions come up, or
- if an inner dialogue is interfering with your observational attitude.

Repetition is also a good idea if the problem is complex or involves a number of people or situations. In that case, you can also change the theme of the sentence according to what comes up. In your observations, pay attention to any changes in images, thoughts, or mood. If you repeat the sentence, examine whether the effect is deepened or strengthened. Then move on to the second sentence.

THE TRANSITION

During the pause, in the few moments after applying Logosynthesis sentences, many people have a sudden sense of a new peace in the room—they can hear a clock ticking or the birds chirping in the garden. Others are struck by the daylight flooding the room.

In summary, formulate the issue accurately into a sentence, repeat sentence 1 and let it sink in for a while. Notice changes in your sense impressions, physical experiences, emotions, thoughts, and beliefs. Also look and listen outwardly and internally. You may not notice the change, because it feels so natural, so *Self-evident*, in the literal sense.

SENTENCE 2: REMOVING NON-ME ENERGY

Sentence 2 usually strengthens the effect of sentence 1. In this phase, the Self removes the introjects of the earlier external world connected to the issue to which you're applying Logosynthesis—energy structures of others and other objects and circumstances frozen within your body and personal space. To do this, use sentence 2, also termed the "removal sentence." In this phase also, you can trust the creative power of the Word. The effect is so astonishing that you need to have experienced the application.

THE SENTENCE

Sentence two, the removal sentence, reads as follows

I remove all non-me energy connected to (event, person, object, place) X from all of my cells, from all of my body, and from my personal space and send it back wherever it belongs.

THE PAUSE IN THE PROCESS

Return to the observational attitude after sentence 2 also. Take a creative break. Let go and relax. Observe your internal processes such as tension, relaxation, pulse rate, body temperature, emotions, thought patterns, and external changes such as—what you hear, see, and feel around your body. Let these experiences pass like clouds in the sky. You don't need to influence them. The power of the Word will do all the work without the control of the conscious ego. The removal sentence is also repeated any time you're losing concentration or emotions or thoughts are impeding your observation.

THE TRANSITION

Many people claim a deeper sense of relaxation following the removal sentence than after the first one, despite thinking they were already very relaxed after the first. At the end of the pause in the process, examine closely the changes in your thinking, emotions, and physicals state. Now find the difference on the distress scale. At this stage, it's not really important whether the symptom or negative emotions have disappeared; what matters is that you notice a change. Sometimes something shows up that is even more disturbing than the original issue. This proves that the process of change has begun, and that the Self grabs the occasion to process more material. You only need to continue it.

THE NEXT STAGE

Usually, there are perceptible changes during any application cycle. Emotional distress may be reduced, or there may be distinctive changes in feelings—sadness may become anger; intense fury may give way to a gentle movement towards reconciliation. The basic issue may take on a different meaning or even be redefined. It is generally worth pursuing new issues that arise. In the current state, the energy flow is often still blocked—even when anger feels better than sadness. When you have negative thoughts about yourself or other people, there still are frozen energy structures around. These prevent you from growing on your personal journey. In such cases, you move to the next cycle, until your stress score comes down to one or even zero.

Following cycles are identical to the ones already outlined. Define the next issue, and then focus carefully on a single aspect that is so minor that it's easy to determine change. Use the salami principle of cutting large chunks into small thin slices. Then formulate and repeat sentence 1 and sentence 2.

INTEGRATION

Again, when you have repeated the sentences and let them sink in, spend some time examining their effect closely. What's different now? How high is the stress-level for this problem now? When you feel satisfied, process another symptom or aspect. Continue until you've neutralised all the historical emotions, thoughts, and environmental aspects you've found, and no new negative thoughts or feelings come up.

Now you have finished processing the current issue and you're ready to integrate the newly processed material. The final step in the procedure is always integration. At this stage, you examine your fresh insight within a daily context. This is the beginning of a different perspective on the issue with which you have been dealing.

As soon as you have defined the symptoms you've been dealing with, you'll be surprised, firstly at your fresh perspective on the issue and secondly, at how it became easier to develop strategies for dealing with the problem. At this stage, many people can think about the treated issue in a matter-of-fact way. For example, you understand your mother-in law and can even understand her behaviour. She now shows an affection for your children you weren't aware of and, admittedly, she has a certain sense of humour even if this isn't yours.

Before you used Logosynthesis, and while you were using it, you may have had the idea that a solution was impossible. Now your focus will be directed towards practical, even day-to-day solutions. Why don't you take a long walk after that celebration dinner?

Sometimes you simply can't imagine how it has taken so long to gain such a simple insight. The problem may not have disappeared by applying Logosynthesis, but it does make a big difference, whether you try to find an adult solution or replay childish patterns like a robot when you initiated those patterns you could find at the time. However, now the world is a different place; you have learned that you can't force others to make you happy, and others can't force you to do the same to them.

Sometimes you need to learn a new language and technique for your new way of being in the world. If you have always avoided conflict you may have never learnt to defend your own interests in a healthy way. You may have even have indulged in reasons to justify your behaviour. You may say that we should avoid conflict or turn the other cheek to enemies. This theory is no longer valid; but do you know how to defend yourself now?

Here, further issues may show up to treat with Logosynthesis. However, it can also mean that you have to learn something new, because you simply don't possess the necessary skills, like taking a course on conflict resolution. In this stage of working on yourself, *future pacing* is the next step. Imagine that next week you find yourself in the same situation that worried you before. Let the various scenes of this video pass before your inner eye one by one. Where does the video roll on and where does it get stuck? If, for example, you were in a conflict with someone at your workplace, imagine that you invite this colleague to a meeting. Ask yourself questions like:

- *How does your colleague react to your invitation?*
- *How will the video continue if he reacts positively?*
- *How will the video continue if he reacts harshly?*

- *How does the arranged meeting go?*
- *At the meeting, can you state your reasons for wanting to discuss the conflict?*
- *Are you able to take your colleague's interests seriously?*
- *Can you find a compromise with your colleague or do you stick to your point of view?*
- *What is your point of view when your colleague refuses to compromise?*
- *How do you deal with it when you're confronted by negative emotions?*

If you can let your inner video play uninterrupted, then you're well prepared for the actual meeting with your colleague. Mostly there will be scenes in which the film gets stuck or fresh negative emotions arise. If you can reflect calmly on a positive solution, take them as the opening of a new processing stage, otherwise take a break, and sleep on it. The resolution may depend on your acceptance of the world and the people as they are, *sans rancune*, without a narcissistic desire to change them.

3.4.
Applying Logosynthesis

As I developed Logosynthesis, and the effectiveness of the method slowly became clear, there were no professionals who could help me to work on my own issues. I had no alternative but to apply the method to myself and to practice each new step until I had found the most simple, elegant, and effective form. In time, I applied it in many areas of my life. Dissolving frozen worlds freed up a lot of energy and helped me to refocus this energy. Even afterwards, it had a surprising effect. While I was on holiday in France recently, I was surprised at how fluently I could express myself in French, which was really a challenge to me before. Processing events from the time I was learning French had given me renewed access to its words and grammar.

Applying Logosynthesis to oneself is somewhat paradoxical—to reintegrate fragments of the Self you need to split off a part of you to set the process in motion. Not everybody is able to do this, especially in the beginning. The more you practice, however, the more fluent the sentences for dissolving earlier patterns and reintegrating their energy will become. With experience, you'll become increasingly skilled at it, especially because Logosynthesis really works "by itself."

The more free energy you have available for the process, the easier it will be to look at your issues and recognise them as frozen thought patterns.

This vital, restorative spiral can go on indefinitely. Life itself will bring many unpleasant experiences to the surface that still influence your perception of your present world. When working on your personal issues, it's important to pick a quiet moment in peaceful surroundings and concentrate fully on the process. Prepare your work well. List the issues you want to process such as beliefs, emotions, desires, and plans. Write down the sentences to help you. Then read the sentences aloud and let them sink in. Then observe the effect.

AREAS OF APPLICATION

You can apply Logosynthesis in all areas of your life. You can relieve suffering, reduce anxiety, neutralise distressing experiences, or clarify your purpose in life. Logosynthesis has also been tested on exam nerves. Sportspeople have learnt to overcome defeat, musicians lost stage fright, and many found a perspective on their career and relationships. The four axioms relate to all of these areas because they apply to life itself. You'll soon notice that in the progress of time, you're gaining an ever-increasing awareness of your talents and life purpose.

This section of the book will provide you with practical recommendations for the issues in your own life. If you remember, Axiom 1—being and suffering—has four basic causes of losing contact with your Self in the here-and-now.

1. Negative experiences in the past
2. Positive experiences in the past
3. Negative experiences in the future
4. Positive experiences in the future

What does this mean?

1. Negative past experiences are stored in frozen worlds. During your childhood or even later in life, there have been events that you couldn't process, and you stored the accompanying emotions, thoughts, and sensory experiences in your energy system. Each time a similar event occurs, you respond with identical emotions and thoughts: shame, sadness, fury, annoyance, or disgust. The old thoughts are reactivated; they generally revolve around powerlessness and vulnerability, or around the opposite—the desire to put others in the victim position. Another expression of a frozen past is indifference—"It's none of my concern"— though it could be of great benefit to yourself and others if you purposefully set about the task. It speaks for itself that the reactions that originate from these patterns are not especially appropriate if you want to make a fresh start in life. The first set of applications of Logosynthesis is concerned with this area.
2. Positive experiences in the past can hinder and block access to the present in exactly the same way as negative ones. When I was seventeen and my great love had given me up, my father tried to comfort me by saying, "There are plenty more fish in the sea." That wasn't a very sensitive remark, and I was furious—just how could he wound my soul so deeply? Now, many years later, I see that he was basically right—there's no sense in holding on to positive past experiences. Real life is in the here-and-now, with the full potential of Essence. Frozen memories may contain positive feelings as much as negative ones.

We must retrieve the energy we have bound up in them and free it for our Self in the here-and-now, where we need it. Only then can we make progress on our life's journey. This area of application is especially important in interpersonal relationships. If we hold onto positive feelings from the past, we will ignore or devalue opportunities offered in the present. As long as you're grieving the loss of a beloved person, you don't see all the ones who love you now.

3. Negative experiences in the future only exist as fantasies. They are based on the illusion that an emotionally distressing past will continue into the future. An former boss of mine liked to quote a poem by the poet Nicolaas Beets that I've translated loosely from Dutch into the following:

A man suffers most from the pain

that the thinks he sees approaching,

but never appears.

Thus he has more to bear

than God gave him to carry.

Logosynthesis helps to reduce the fear of negative experiences in the future.

4. Positive experiences in the future can be excluded from one's own influence. When my wife, Luzia, and myself were taking a trip in a horse-drawn carriage through the Egyptian city of Luxor, we asked the Arabic driver whether he owned the horse and carriage. He said he didn't. He had hired them from

a man who owned a large number of them. Then we asked him whether he ever intended to have a carriage of his own. He answered me with a typical Arabic gesture, throwing his hands towards Heaven and said, "Insh'allah," "God will decide." When I asked what he himself could contribute, he again replied "Insh'allah."

Our driver will never have his own carriage. Why not? He is dreaming of a future for which he himself takes no responsibility in the present.

4.
Areas of Application

The following section describes the principal areas of application for Logosynthesis. With the help of the basic procedure, you can work on a large number of issues. The more specific you can be with regard to the issues, the more effective Logosynthesis will be. Some issues will be easier to handle than others. There is no fundamental difference in treating the various symptoms and states. Emotional, physical, cognitive, and relationship problems are all caused by the disconnection from Essence in the here-and-now. Logosynthesis will dissolve frozen energy constructs and re-establish the connection. Over time, specific applications will be established in the various areas. The ideas expressed here about applying Logosynthesis to yourself aren't set in stone. Take them as a beginning, an inspiration to open your Self.

4.1.
Fear

Emotions add colour to our lives. In our culture, they play an extremely important role in meeting others and ourselves. Many of us allow our emotions to guide our actions.

From a biological standpoint, emotions are purely directed to aspects of our environment that require immediate reaction. Fear points to danger; anger indicates that that our boundaries have been violated; shame or guilt confronts us with the fact that we have broken societal conventions.

Fear is the dread of possible suffering based on a present or prospective threat. Fear is the biological activation of the body to deal with a present physical and biological threat such as hunger, thirst, or danger in our surroundings; it may also relate to the threat of abandonment or separation from society. Insofar as these risks are conceivable, we speak of fear. The fear of illness, violence, death, war, intimidation, the loss of someone close, or losing material possessions may be founded on realistic expectations. They may also be a fantasy—incomprehensible and/or unfounded in concrete terms. When such a fear assumes a serious form, we talk about a phobia—a fear of department stores, lifts, mice, spiders, or other people. Our fear is not mainly based on the actual threat in our present surroundings; it is founded on imprints stored many years earlier in our personal space. Here is one example:

Luzia, my wife, accompanied me one Sunday on a trip to a historic site across a steep, narrow mountain road. A sign at the start of the road warned of falling stones. As we moved along, Luzia seemed anxious. When I asked what was the matter, she replied that on a recent trip on that road, a boulder had come loose from the wall and fallen out in front of her. Afterwards, herself and her passenger had to push the boulder off the road. Now she feared that the same thing could happen again. This everyday incident contains all the essential elements of fear as a biological warning mechanism in itself:

- Something occurred.
- The incident involved an element of danger.
- Luzia survived the incident without damage.
- She is expecting something similar to happen in the future, given the same set of circumstances.

Here it's not important whether there was actual injury or harm in the past, or whether Luzia imagines it to be so. When it comes to examining potentially dangerous situations, our brain makes no distinction between real situations and fantasies about everything that could have happened. Both will activate our internal warning system in future potentially dangerous situations.

For physical threats, this learning strategy makes sense. The saying goes that if a child gets burnt, he'll be afraid of fire, and rightly so. Experience teaches us to protect ourselves. It only causes problems when our brain sends out alarm signals not related to the real threat in a situation.

FEAR AND LOGOSYNTHESIS

In terms of Logosynthesis, fears are thought forms. When you're experiencing fear, this sounds coolly detached. To dissolve fear, you need to realise that most emotions are archaic, frozen thought forms. Your fear can seem very real when your entire biology is organised to survive the perceived danger. Your brain's limbic system is in a state of alarm, stress hormones are released, and you oscillate between fight, flight, and freezing. The brain cannot make a "rational" decision. Since the beginning of evolution, this reaction has protected us from danger. Since then, however, changes have taken place. In the past, we were exposed to dangers like hunger, thirst, cold, and wild animals. Nowadays, we are more likely to be overfed and the wild animals need to be protected against us rather than the other way round.

Our biological reaction patterns are no longer triggered by real, present dangers, but much more by imaginary ones. If a sinister type looms in front of you in a dark alley with a knife in his hand, the fight-flight-freeze programme in your brain is quite meaningful; you decide in an instant whether you should run away, struggle, or give up. These reactions are equally triggered by the memory of unprocessed, dangerous incidents, even when the threat is long since past. Fear is an important area of application for Logosynthesis. Archaic fears dissolve when we re-establish contact with our Self and our emotions reassume their initial significance as a warning mechanism in the here-and-now. With Logosynthesis, there are two staring points in working with fears:

1. Fear is usually fixed in a frozen fragment. This part will be reintegrated into the Self.
2. Imprints of a situation perceived as threatening are connected to this archaic part. The energy of these imprints will be removed from the body and personal space.

Old fears disappear without a trace when the energy is retrieved from the old fragment to the Self, and the frozen energy of the environment is removed from our own body and personal space. Retrieving the energy from the old fragments strengthens the living, active Self. The person feels enabled to remove imprints previously seen as powerful. This provides a better way of coping with dangers in the here-and-now. To remove energy from old parts, four types of frozen world need to be treated:

1. The *first* experience. The first experience of the fear forms the basis for the pattern. All other experiences reinforce the effects of the first experience. However, the effect of later experiences will be diminished as soon as the initial experience has been neutralised.
2. The *worst* experience. In most cases, the worst experience has strengthened our reaction pattern. Dissolving the frozen world of this experience removes the latter's sharp edges and starts the healing process.
3. The *most recent* experience. The experience that occurred in the most recent past is rooted in the earlier patterns. Yet it gives the most vivid illusion of reality because it is so close to adult consciousness.

Working with the latest experience establishes the difference between past and present.

4. The *next expected experience*. The memory of the three previous experiences forms the basis of the illusion that the future will also hold threatening experiences. In terms of energy, there is no difference between memories and fantasies. A fantasy is just as powerful as any memory in triggering the biological reactions described.

In the treatment for fear, we dissolve the dissociated parts and imprints connected to the four aspects above.

Here are the steps in applying Logosynthesis to yourself.

1. Find some free space to apply the technique.
2. Follow the start-up procedure.
3. Specify and focus on the fear to which you want to apply Logosynthesis.
4. Estimate the level of distress caused by the fear
5. Formulate the sentences, repeat them, and leave sufficient time for them to sink in.
6. Re-estimate the level of distress caused by the fear.
7. Continue with the next step.

CLEARING A SPACE

Find a free space before you start to work with Logosynthesis. Make sure that you're in a comfortable environment and that nothing will distract you. In working with fear, it's important that people feel secure. If you're not feeling confident, ask someone to support you. In this case, it is important that your companion has also read this book so that they can follow the steps along with you. You never need to work on your own.

If you'd like to work on major issues and don't feel confident, it's better to consult a trained professional. You will find a list on www.logosyntheis.net.

SPECIFYING AND FOCUSING

Before you begin to apply Logosynthesis, put your experiences of fear in order. In addition, write down a number of fear-provoking experiences. It's best to describe each experience on an index card. Later you will find it easier to put them in order. In each case, note the first, worst, and most recent occurrence. Include on your list the next expected situation. When you have a list or pile of cards write down for each experience:

- *What alarms you most in this situation? Something you see, hear, feel, smell, or taste?*
- *Where is the frightening person or object in your personal space? How far away are they? Are they in front of you, behind you, to your left or right, above, or below you?*
- *How do you react internally to this person or object? What are your emotions? What are your physical sensations? What are your thoughts? What are your fantasies?*

Now place your list or pile of cards in chronological order. Begin with the earliest experience and continue up to the present. The result will be a so-called hierarchy of fears, for example:

1. *Getting stuck in a lift*
2. *Being locked in a room*
3. *Travelling by car through a long tunnel*
4. *Taking a lift on your own*
5. *Travelling on a crowded cable car*
6. *Travelling by train*
7. *Getting stuck in a garment because the zipper is jammed*
8. *Travelling in the back of a two-door car*
9. *Wearing a tight ring on your finger*

THE DISTRESS EXPERIENCED

The SUD scale I described earlier will help you to establish how the distress attached to symptoms of fear changes over time. If you want to work with the fear of sitting in the back of a two-door car, you rate the distress connected to this fear on a scale of zero to ten. A score of zero signifies no fear. A score of ten represents a fear that is extremely stressful. Then treat the issue and rate the stress again. Note the issues and the scores. For example:

Sitting in the back of a two-door car

0 ———————————————————— 10
X

Carry out the technique. After you have let the sentences sink in, remember the scene again, and examine how high the stress rating is. The scale will then appear like this, for example:

Sitting in the back of a two-door car

0 10

X

In most cases, the score goes down a few points on the stress scale. Is it also possible that a new, more stressful issue may emerge while the original one becomes less significant? In this case, draw up a second scale and rate the distress coming from this new issue:

Driving through a tunnel in a convertible

0 10

X

Creating several scales will allow you to work on several issues simultaneously without losing perspective. The objective is that, eventually, each of your scales should shift as a close as possible to zero. You can apply this tool to any issue. It's especially useful when you're having difficulty in assessing your own internal state.

Note that your SUD scale refers to the distress you're feeling because of a particular symptom at a certain moment. It's not a question of the strength or intensity of the symptom itself. This distinction is especially important in physical complaints. If, for example, you have a headache, it may be just as bad after a session of Logosynthesis, but it may cause you less subjective distress. Now apply the scale to the various issues in your pile and afterwards reorganise the pile. The card describing the event or aspect that bothers you least should be on the top of the pile. As you continue to apply Logosynthesis, the pile may diminish.

LOGOSYNTHESIS APPLIED TO FEAR

Don't force anything. That would be counterproductive. You can try to jump up the stairs four steps at once, but if you want to get to the top intact, it's better to take one step after the other. You've had the problem for a long time already, and doesn't matter whether your symptoms are eliminated today or next week. It matters whether you can live your life free of fear in the long term. With Logosynthesis, courage is misplaced. Begin with the least anxiety-provoking experience in the pile. The SUD scale will enable you to do this. Start with issues that you have rated at six or below on the scale.

Now you have an issue on which you can formulate sentences. Take, as an example, the fear of sitting in the back of a car with the additional factor that the driver is forced to brake when another car approaches from the right. Imagine you've rated this as a six. In this case, the sentences are as follows:

1. *I retrieve all my energy bound up in the fear of sitting in the back of a two-door car while the driver is forced to brake back to the right place in my Self.*
2. *I remove all non-me energy connected to the fear of sitting in the back of a two-door car while the driver is forced to brake from all of my cells, from all of my body, and from my personal space, and send it back to wherever it belongs.*

A SECOND RATING OF SUBJECTIVE DISTRESS

After the application, you will probably feel a slight change or a feeling of relief. Refer back to your notes on the stress scale.

Sitting in the back of a two-door car

0 ——————————————— Y —— X ——————————————— 10

X represents the first estimate and Y the second. If your internal images have changed, you'll find the latter now scored lower on the SUD scale. If your score is the same, investigate the difference in your internal images connected to the fear. To continue the example of the two-door car, instead of the image of the driver of the two-door braking, an image has emerged of a person wanting to get out of the car, but who is unable to find the lever to raise the front seat. People frequently change quickly and unconsciously to another theme or aspect.

When you have repeated a sentence and let it sink in, details of the introjects in your personal space will change. The colour, distance, direction, or density of the images may change. If they do, your reaction to them will change correspondingly. For this reason, the focusing stage is important—establish your issue as exactly as possible and find the location of the introjects in space. This will help you to notice changes, even minor ones.

THE NEXT ELEMENT

The next aspect may originate from the work itself. You may, for example, experience a physical symptom such as a racing heart, pressure in your head, fatigue, or dizziness. Such reactions constitute the basis for the next stage in of the application technique. Once again, formulate two sentences:

1. *I retrieve all my energy bound up in this dizziness to the right place within my Self.*
2. *I remove all non-me energy connected to this dizziness from all of my cells, from all of my body, and from my personal space, and send it back to wherever it belongs.*

When the stress rating of the earlier traumatic situation has been reduced to one or zero, and no further traumatic images or experiences arise, take a break. During the break, drink a few glasses of water to replenish your body in the process. Then take the next card from your pile. As a rule, don't spend more than forty or fifty minutes a day at Logosynthesis. It is important to realise that your thoughts, feelings, and actions need to adjust to a new state.

INTENSE EMOTIONS

Intense emotions often arise when you're beginning to work with Logosynthesis. Some people think that things are just getting worse and they give up. Here there are several possibilities. When you begin to apply Logosynthesis, you still haven't realised that negative emotions due to past experiences are actually just energy structures triggered by external influences. Observe each emotion in its own right and apply the relevant sentences. After a while, your free energy will be raised and your Self will take over. You'll need to identify less with the archaic, frozen worlds. In the beginning, your ego will tend to identify yourself with your emotions. Your Self will always know that this is not the case. If your emotions prove too painful and you don't feel confident enough to continue the work, consult a trained professional. He or she can provide the security you need to carry out the process.

VISUALISING THE FUTURE

Future pacing, imagining a situation in the immediate future where the fear could arise again, decides whether the treatment has been adequate. If you can remain calm while you imagine a previously stressful situation, you will normally tolerate it calmly when it does happen. If it turns out in the future that aspects of the fear are still there, this generally means that not all the trigger situations have been resolved.

SHAME

Shame is a special form of fear. This emotion is linked to very strong frozen fragments from childhood. People in shame feel like a small child who is being disciplined and knows they've broken the rules. Indications of shame are:

- losing eye contact;
- disordered thoughts, confusion, disorientation;
- speech disorders, stammering, stuttering;
- feeling very small;
- self-preoccupation; and
- submissiveness, co-dependency.

In its disguised form, shame may reveal itself as self-importance and arrogance. Shame is a dissociated state with strong beliefs and extremely powerful introjects.

SHAME AND LOGOSYNTHESIS

In working with shame, it is very important to examine the beliefs and introjects at its roots. You'll notice shame if you transgressed inner rules of which you were not aware. When you trace back these rules, you will remember experiences in which parental figures have punished you or exposed your bad behaviour in front of others. Logosynthesis needs to neutralise the memory of such incident. Only then will you be able to judge whether these rules were as generally valid as you had previously assumed. While working with shame especially, it is worth examining the location and expression of punitive parental figures in your personal space as a start. Where are these figures located in space? In front of you, behind you, to your left, to your right, above, or below you? How far away from you? What are their facial and physical expressions? Your replies to these questions will help you to identify accurately changes that occur during the application of Logosynthesis, even if the emotions haven't dissolved immediately.

4.2. Rage, Anger and Forgiveness

BEING OUTSIDE OF YOURSELF

Rage and anger have enormous consequences on our communication with others. Biologically, they are a reaction to a threat, like fear, and part of the fight-flight reaction in the brain's limbic system, the "reptile brain." Rage and anger belong to the survival mode; their function is to keep our enemies at bay. Rage prepares us to use force to defend ourselves, our kin, and our territory.

In everyday life, rage and anger in their original biological form are barely useful. In a society that depends on the communication skills of its members, such emotions are usually inappropriate. The direct expression of rage and anger tends to escalate and seldom resolves existing conflicts. Logosynthesis changes the perspective of the angry person and helps him to protect his own interests without disregarding those of others.

An important, practical problem with rage and anger is that the person concerned sees them as justified, even when their expression appears exaggerated and even destructive to everyone else. Rage and anger are aspects of the Apparently Normal Personality and serve as a compensation for hurt and abandonment. This is further illustrated by the fact that many people in the grip of this emotion quickly change their attitude when they experience the other person as taking them seriously.

Role models for rage and anger usually come from an introject. They replace the original pain repressed from awareness—the Apparently Normal Personality. If you work with anger and rage, identify your role model and examine where exactly he or she is located in your personal space. Use sentence 1 to retrieve your energy and then observe the change in the introject. Then use sentence 2 to remove the energy connected to the role model from your cells, your body, and from your personal space, and send it back to wherever it belongs. Then observe what remains of the image of the representation of the role model.

Rage and anger often become issues for people in a process of change, when they let go of their Emotional Personality with all its injuries. They discover that at an earlier stage in their life, they were not able to set clear, sufficient boundaries.

Many emotions closely associated with past events are now irrelevant. Clients must retrieve their energy from archaic rage and anger, however justified they may seem. Only the retrieval of our own energy from the person and the situation will create freedom in the here-and-now. This means forgiveness. In dealing with rage and anger, forgiveness is not simply an altruistic act but rather a tool for psychic hygiene—I return the responsibility for his actions to the object of my rage and go my own fresh path.

FORGIVENESS

It makes no difference whether archaic rage and irritation are repressed or expressed. In both cases, we dissociate parts of our consciousness as either the Emotional

Personality or the Apparently Normal Personality. Both patterns weaken contact with Essence. Good health, satisfying work, and loving relationships are only possible if our energy is flowing freely. Forgiveness frees us from the tunnel vision of the past. We cleanse our energy system and reconnect with Essence, our living Self. Forgiveness creates better conditions for the future than rage and anger. Using Logosynthesis, the following exercise will help you to forgive.

1. Imagine meeting the person who hurt you.
2. Notice your emotions when you think of the damage or injury you suffered. Take all your energy bound up in these emotions back to the right place in yourself.
3. Allow yourself to notice all fantasies you connect with this person. The desire to tell them to go jump in a lake might perhaps be the most harmless. Take all your energy connected to these fantasies back to the right place in yourself.
4. Examine what you have lost through your involvement with this person. Take all your energy from the sadness and this loss back to the right place in yourself.
5. Examine all the expectations you had of this person. Take all your energy from these expectations back to the right place in yourself.
6. Examine everything you expect of yourself in this situation. Take all your energy from these expectations back to the right place in yourself.
7. Finally, remove all the other person's energy from your cells, from your entire body, and from your personal space, and send it back to wherever it really belongs.

After applying the basic procedure of Logosynthesis a number of times, you probably will be able to reassess the situation and change your own behaviour. If, however, you don't have a sense of equilibrium and relaxation, there will be, as yet, untreated aspects. Beneath these experiences, even earlier painful experiences may lie dormant, which are activated by that person. Take the time to uncover the earlier experiences and repeat the procedure with them.

4.3.
Relationships

"It is not good for man to be alone," states the first Book of Genesis. God saw the problem and solved it for Adam by creating Eve. This was the beginning of a long story, which proved that the problem couldn't be solved for once and for all.

Relationships have important biological and mental functions, some of which are directly opposed to others. They are in a permanent state of tension between stability and change. If there is too much stability, we become bored. If there is too little, it makes us insecure. It follows that relationships are very susceptible to dissociative mechanisms. Real, living relationships only exist in the here-and-now. Dissociation and introjection impede true awareness of the other.

Nowadays, every second or third marriage ends in divorce. One would expect people to learn from their experiences, and that the prognosis for second marriages would be better. This is not so. This shows that people do change their partners, but not the patterns that cause their marriage to break down. There are several reasons for that. The main one is that people are not with their partner as their Self in the present. Instead, the patterns of previous failed relationships are continuing. Working with Logosynthesis, I have found six destructive relationship patterns:

1. Transference
2. Trauma
3. Illusions
4. Fantasies
5. Idealising
6. Fear.

These categories may help you to identify frozen aspects of your own relationships. Logosynthesis may help you to eliminate these negative aspects. It will open your eyes to the people you're close to at present. The patterns generally emerges in combination with one another.

1. Transference
   This pattern exists always and everywhere. You see your partner unconsciously as someone else from your own history. You don't perceive the other as he or she really is and expect the partner to behave like the figure from your past—in the positive or in the negative. You will tend to react to your partner in the same way as to the historical figure. That works as a trigger, and your partner will show exactly the same, familiar thoughts, feelings, and behaviour.

2. Trauma
   In every relationship, emotional injuries and wounds are caused when a partner consciously or unconsciously ignores or dismisses the other person's needs. Expectations stay unfulfilled and the couple confront one another defensively. Each is frozen in the dissociated state of the moment of the emotional

injury, of contempt, or unfaithfulness. They let go of their expectations. The relationship cannot grow any further and remains stuck in the experience of the injury.

3. Longing for the lost ideal
   Every successful relationship begins with the stage of idealising the other. Strengths are exaggerated and weaknesses ignored. In a healthy relationship, this idealised image is replaced, as time goes on, by a realistic view of the partner. If this doesn't happen, the relationship will be frozen as the partner is continuously longing for the lost ideal. The person will cling to the romantic image of the partner, which has no relevance to the person they are with now. The development of the relationship, and those involved, come to a stop.

4. Wishes
   You want your partner to fulfil your wishes, and you tend to ignore your partner's own true capabilities, desires, and needs. During the infatuation stage, the partner will easily read your desires in your eyes. In everyday life, this becomes more and more difficult. It gets to a point where the partner discovers that this adapting attitude leads to deficits for him or herself. In the long run, such fantasies will destroy your relationship.

5. Idealising and projection
   If you idealise your partner, you're inevitably out of touch with Essence. Instead, you exaggerate the

qualities of the partner, whose personality or presence is especially associated with extreme happiness. This means you will become dependent on your partner. Dependency will lead to loss of interest in you.

6. Fear
   In this pattern, there is a fear that something will happen to the partner and the person will be left alone and helpless. They disregard their own Essence and surrender their power and strengths.

Relationships that follow these patterns hold you back from developing your relationship or marriage. They prevent you from letting go of earlier relationships and starting new ones that could bring you more fulfilment.

LOGOSYNTHESIS IN RELATIONSHIPS

Because of the patterns described above, relationships are the primary theatres of dissociation and introjection. This is almost impossible to prevent. Applying Logosynthesis can be a great help, but there are some pitfalls here. Logosynthesis starts from a different perspective than most approaches, and its pragmatic attitude can cause resistance. That attitude is aimed at reconnecting with the Self. This contrasts to the romantic ideal that we should do what we can to make one another happy. In practice, the opposite is true. When the powerful frozen worlds are resolved, you and your partner will both emerge into the here-and-now. As partners, you will then become a great deal more attractive for each other than frozen images could ever be. This implies, however, that both assume responsibility for your Selves, and that means you cannot hand it over to anyone else. You create your own luck in the truest sense. However, applying Logosynthesis can also cause open your eyes to see that you've married your mother or father. You may have fostered unrealistic expectations of your partner over the years. This man or woman will never live up to them.

Work in the area of couple-relationships is not straightforward, for a number of reasons:

- The break-up of a couple's relationship seldom actually takes place in the here-and-now. On both sides, there are introjects of parents, brothers and sisters, and earlier relationships. These are supported and strengthened by authority figures from the church, politics, and society. They activate dissociated parts, which obscure your view of each other as you really are.
- Relationships easily activate patterns of dependency. This makes it difficult to separate without guilt.
- Our western culture puts big demands on relationships. They are supposed to provide a source of happiness, action, and stability. This culture is expressed through films, songs, and many books offering advice.
- Every relationship has a subtle power balance. Any intervention can disrupt this and deepen the insecurity on both sides.

If you want to change your relationship to the positive, it makes good sense to proceed cautiously. A constructive relationship pattern is not made in a day, and you need two people to create it.

DEVELOPMENT THROUGH RELATIONSHIPS

If you want to use Logosynthesis to change your life, you can start with your relationship. It can enable you to take responsibility for yourself in the communication with your partner. It's not a problem if you're single at the moment. You can begin to eliminate any memories from the past, as well as expectations of any future relationships. If you do, you'll have higher chance of meeting your mate. Don't try to clear at once all the patterns that are disturbing you. Take one step at a time as you would in any other area. Here, also, it's important to work with aspects rather than with the whole person. You need to dissolve frozen romantic images of dream relationships, dream honeymoons, and unresolved separations. At first glance, it seems counterintuitive and irresponsible to resolve connections to positive experiences and images. Working on relationships, however, means exactly this—relationships are enacted in the here-and-now, and the only real source of energy is in the present, not in long gone honeymoons. Only if you let go of the past, negative or positive, with this person or another, can you create an opportunity for happiness and growth—now. Logosynthesis will lead to a fresh insight into yourself, into your Self, and your life, for both partners.

Every day presents plenty of opportunities to activate your own Self in the relationship rather than follow frozen patterns. Logosynthesis will give you space for fresh encounters with actual people in the here-and-now. Start the work on your relationship with single aspects. Think of a situation involving your partner that upset you. Examine where your partner's image is located in your personal space or in your body. How far away is it, how big? Then take a minor aspect of this introject and your reaction to it—an image, a thought, an emotion, or a physical sensation:

1. *I retrieve all the energy bound up in aspect X of event Y with person Z and take it back to the right place in my Self.*
2. *I remove all the energy of Z involved in this experience from all of my cells, from my body, and from my personal space, and send it back to the right place in her/his Self.*

This is the way to create space for Essence in your relationship. When both partners are in contact with Essence, their relationship will be truly dynamic. Now they can both help one another to realise their life task.

RELATIONSHIPS IN THE WORKPLACE

What I've already said about couples' relationships applies *mutatis mutandis* to relationships in the workplace with superiors, employees, and colleagues. Similarly, these relationships can only be positive if everyone concerned is in touch with their Essence. This is obviously the perfect situation and, therefore, rare. You can, however, start the process. The quality of relationships in the workplace improves when you yourself take responsibility for your role, tasks and projects within the organisation. If your colleagues stay stuck in the transference, in spite of your efforts, this transference could be positive.

4.4.
Dreams

Dreams are an important area of application of Logosynthesis. Fritz Perls, the founder of Gestalt therapy, assumed that every person and every element in a dream reflects aspects of the dreamer's personality. An example: I have a dream of being on a car journey with my wife. The battery goes dead, the car keys are gone and we can't get out of the parking lot of a service area. There are seven elements in the dream, each one representing a part of myself: the persona in the dream, the car, the battery, my wife, the parking lot, the car keys, and the service area.

In Gestalt therapy, the therapist gets their clients to identify with each of these elements. The result is a role-play in which the various elements enter into dialogue with one another. Using Logosynthesis, such a structured debate with the dream is unnecessary. According to Axiom 2, the objects in the dream are dissociated parts with their corresponding imprints. According to key Axiom 3, they are energy constructs whose purpose is to stabilise our frame of reference. We are, however, according to Axiom 1, Essence, to which all parts can be redirected. It is, therefore, unnecessary, maybe even counterproductive, to reinforce these parts through detailed differentiation. We can just retrieve our frozen energy bound up in them and remove from our system what doesn't belong there.

This is particularly significant when you wake up from a nightmare. You're still experiencing the negative emotions and you're in a state of physical arousal. Your heart is racing, you're sweating, and you're thinking about how you can get out of this mess. To put the dream behind you, make a list of the people, objects, and other elements of the situation in the dream. Note their location in your personal space. In my example they are:

- Myself
- My wife
- The car
- The battery
- The parking lot
- The car keys
- The service area

Then take your energy from all these elements back to your Self and remove the non-you energy invested in these elements. Examine how the representations of people and objects in your personal space change or dissolve. You'll be surprised how your internal state will change in reaction to this process. It is important that you retrieve your own energy as well as remove the non-you energy invested in every element of the dream, including yourself as the key subject in the dream.

Dreams reflect our deep unconscious processes. The conscious ego cannot always comprehend this either. The aim of traditional psychotherapeutic dream work is to increase the consciousness of the ego during the process, based on the Freudian maxim: "Where Id was, there Ego shall be." For Logosynthesis, however, strengthening the ego is not a priority, because the focus of the latter is limited to its earthly environment. It tends to ignore Essence and, therefore, is not really able to solve our life problems.

As soon as the focus of our attention shifts to development of the Self, rather than the ego, the content of dream becomes insignificant. We retrieve the energy bound up in the elements of that content back to the Self. The living Self can then use that energy directly for its own purpose, without any intermediate cognitive steps.

For me, in the dream from the example, working through it with Logosynthesis had an amazing effect. Its symbolism became clear immediately: Essence was telling me that continuing on this path was a dead end. Luzia and I were in a fast-moving environment (the vehicle) which was demanding more energy from us than we could deliver (the battery ran out). Essence sent us the message that it was no option to continue on this road—the key was gone. Of course, there are many alternative interpretations of the dream, but this one fit immediately.

If you have a dream and want to use the dream for your personal development, use the following technique:

- List the people, objects, and other elements in the dream.
- Retrieve your energy from all elements and from yourself as the subject of the dream.
- Remove the non-you energy of these parts from your system.

This can help you rid yourself of the residual effects of a nightmare. It can also reveal the deeper significance of your dreams. Besides, you'll notice your body will reward you with sensations of relaxation and relief in return for your dream work.

If you're finding it difficult to keep your concentration on applying the technique, use a pen and paper to follow the procedure. You may also ask a friend to help you find elements and to formulate the sentences. Logosynthesis isn't memory training, and you have nothing to prove.

After you made your list of elements, compose type one and type two sentences for each element of the dream. Then work with the elements on your list, one by one. Relax and observe the effect on your body, mind, and spirit.

If you're experiencing nightmares following a traumatic experience, it's best to consult a trained professional.

4.5.
Physical Symptoms

The body is an interesting phenomenon. It is the mediator between our Self and the Earth Life System. Our only awareness of our physical environment comes via our senses, and the body enables us to move through space. Most of the time, many of us forget the faithful servant in the background. We gain pleasure from our physical desires. The body provides physical or sexual achievement. It may also constitute an obstacle to the fulfilment of our life task or desires.

Highest pleasure and deepest frustration are closely connected to our physical sensations. The mountaineer, scaling a sheer slope without a rope, is depending on the strength and dexterity of his fingers and toes. He concentrates fully until he reaches the summit. Tennis players like Roger Federer and Rafael Nadal attain an amazing level of perfection on the court; lovers consummate their union through each of the senses; the gourmet savours a sumptuous seven-course meal.

On the other hand, the reality is that our bodies are imperfect. We mature and come into our prime. Later on, beauty, strength, and speed decline. In the end, we each face death. For most of us, our body functions like a perfect machine for a certain period in our life. Sooner or later, however, we will suffer from acute or chronic physical symptoms—life is finite and the body is not perfect. Depending on how we see the world, we adopt one of several views of the body and its functions:

- My body is a complex physiochemical biological machine serving my goals. Injuries or deficiencies can be treated by chemical or technical intervention. Tradesmen, sportsmen, or soldiers tend to think like this.
- Fate determines the body I've been given and I can resist or accept it.
- My body is a window on the world. It helps me to take part in what's going on around me and react to it.
- My body is a manifest energy form and follows the same rules as other energy forms. It is an instrument of my indestructible Essence.

How you regard your body affects your way of coping with illnesses and symptoms.

THE BODY AND HEALING

Healing through Logosynthesis always comprises several elements that may be employed in a variety of ways:

1. The physiological or functional symptom *per se*
2. The degree of limitation the symptom imposes on day-to-day living and the fulfilment of the perceived life task
3. Knowledge of, and beliefs about, the symptoms and the treatments available
4. Dissociation and introjection due to emotional distress caused by the symptom and the emotional acceptance of it

Each of the factors above has an impact on the development and healing of symptoms.

1. The physiological or functional symptom
   The level of suffering is only partially determined by symptoms. For a number of years, I worked at a pulmonary rehabilitation centre located at high altitude. I often wondered about the differences between people. One young man, who still could easily climb the highest mountains around, suffered intensely because of his illness although it was relatively mild. He was comparing himself to other men in his age group. By comparison, one elderly woman was proud to be able to climb the stairs to the third floor of the building, without help, and appreciate the wonderful panoramic vista of the mountains from her window. A physical symptom by itself does not predict the degree of suffering. Patients with chronic diseases often adjust very well, while for others, the limitations placed on day-to-day living predominate.

2. The degree of limitation
   The extent of the limitation imposed on our well-being by a physical symptom is both physical and psychological. Context also plays a part. The same eye condition poses different problems for the assistant who can't work on the computer anymore and the young mother; the former will have to retrain, while the latter will have little difficulty in continuing to be a mother to her children. The extent of physical limitation is also determined by a sense of loss or grief. A biker who can no longer participate in his favourite sport or working life after an accident will probably suffer more from an accident than someone who can continue to engage in meaningful activity.

3. Knowledge of the symptom and its treatment
   Knowledge of the symptom can work in two different directions. On the one hand, it may help you to come to grips with it since you know how to manage your lifestyle and cope in a crisis. The treatment of chronic lung disease or diabetes is enormously simplified for a patient who is well informed about the illness and treatment options. On the other hand, our knowledge of the symptom defines the way we see treatment options. Many people interpret a cancer diagnosis as a death sentence.

4. Dissociation, introjection, and the body
   Our body must interact freely with it our environment. If you have an introject that does let you know that you have to work hard, but not when you're allowed to stop, your health will be in trouble sooner or later. To allow our physical energy to heal our body, we need to leave introjects, emotional wounds, and illnesses behind us. Then our body will become an open unobstructed vehicle for the flow of the Self and your task in the Earth Life System. As long as you hold onto anger, hatred, and resentment towards those who've let you down or injured, you are contaminating and punishing yourself and not that other person. You weaken your immune system, become prone to illness, and reinforce your introjects and dissociated states.

Logosynthesis does not claim to be able to heal the body. It is no substitute for treatment by conventional or alternative medicine. It can, however, ease suffering by activating a process that enables you to see your body and physical symptoms differently. An altered perception can help you to adapt the demands on your own body, end destructive habits, or consider further treatment options.

It is, however, a good idea to use Logosynthesis to treat physical symptoms, especially if they're vague ones, difficult to diagnose or treat by the usual methods. For example, a woman who consulted me had been suffering from vertigo for years. After two sessions, the vertigo was gone.

At times, we can treat physical symptoms, illnesses, and problems effectively and rid ourselves of them. In other cases, we are forced to accept our physical limitations; we may have to acknowledge that our body is trying to tell us something important about our lifestyle. By holding us back, our body teaches us a lesson. Working with Logosynthesis means we have to separate the physical symptoms from other factors. Seldom does a symptom disappear when we simply retrieve our energy from it. Physical elements result from a longer lasting loss of awareness of the Self. Normally, they can be only partially eliminated, not immediately, but after some time. So if you want to influence the healing process, it's better to examine and treat the thoughts and feelings connected to the physical problems. They can be dealt with before trying to treat the actual symptoms and their origins. Adequate coping with symptoms can offer considerable relief.

EMOTIONS AND PHYSICAL SYMPTOMS

Physical illnesses are closely linked to emotions: panic, fear, shame, anger, disgust, or grief. These emotions appear not only in ourselves, but in others too. The emotional problem usually outweighs the physical one and can be a good starting point when applying Logosynthesis to a physical illness. It's usually easier to influence the emotional factors. The body's healing chances improve if the energy bound up in archaic parts is allowed to flow freely. Archaic emotions can be introjected, as well as dissociated.

Loss of a physical capacity or worsening of a symptom may reactivate previous losses and injuries. If people have an illness that has caused great upset to those around them, worries, irritations, and disappointments are likely to be present as imprints. This happens especially with chronic conditions that demand significant adaptation from the sufferer as well as those close to him or her.

BELIEFS AND PHYSICAL SYMPTOMS

Physical conditions are not only connected to powerful emotions, but also to strong beliefs. The latter may be evident as an introject or a dissociated part. Serious illness exceeds our ability to cope with our life situation. That means we create security through dissociation and introjection. If we're ill and can't make sense of our situation, we're inclined to accept any interpretation of our circumstances and hardly question it. What doctors, parents, family members, and friends say has authority beyond the extent of their knowledge.

These authorities, however, don't always have a solution. They too have powerful needs, thoughts, beliefs, expectations, and desires. These complicate our own attitude about our illness or physical suffering.

Applying Logosynthesis to beliefs about the body and illness is no different than treating any other conviction. It is, nevertheless, important to examine closely and focus on each aspect.

The process begins with the type of symptom and its changeability. There are hardly any unchangeable truths about illness and healing. Many ideas are determined by introjects that have never been analysed, such as:

- *Nobody can cure cancer.*
- *Everybody in our family is overweight.*
- *Asthma is inherited and you can do nothing about it.*

Introjects like these reveal clear views on the nature, significance, and changeability of the body, its organs, and its conditions. It is worth examining them more closely and using Logosynthesis to eliminate beliefs relating to the changeability of symptoms.

Treatment options vary, and along with them medications. Stomach ulcers are no longer considered a result of stress, but rather signs of an an infection with *helicobacter pylori*. There have been huge advances in cancer treatment and expert opinions, recommending consumption of eggs, red wine, and coffee, change like the weather. Beliefs contain frozen worlds and it is worth eliminating them using Logosynthesis. Then you'll be able to find a new direction with your eyes and ears wide open.

Simply examine the human body in general and your own in particular. What do you know about?

- *The heart and circulation?*
- *The brain?*
- *The nervous system?*
- *The immune system?*
- *The lungs?*
- *The digestion?*
- *The muscles and skeleton?*
- *The glands?*
- *The reproductive organs?*
- *The kidneys and bladder?*

At the end, ask yourself how long you've known this and who gave you this information. If you find that those sources aren't logical or quite up-to-date, apply the following sentences to the relevant imprint and the emotions connected to it:

1. *I retrieve all my energy bound up in this belief about my body and take it back to the right place in my Self.*
2. *I remove all non-me energy connected to this belief from all of my cells, from my body, and from my personal space, and send it back to wherever it belongs.*

IDENTITY AND SYMPTOMS

We tend to think we are our body. We identify with our physical strength, mobility, agility, and beauty—or with the lack of these qualities. Identifying with the body ignores that we are a mind, and that we are Essence. Identifying with our body creates dissociative states connected to powerful introjects. We can also ask ourselves whether those around us have responded to our being, our Self, or rather to our appearance and physical achievements. The more our adult identity has been characterised by physical qualities and achievements, the stronger the dissociative aspect. A top sportsman who has always had complete confidence in his physical strength will have to reconsider his identity at a certain stage in his life when his strength fails. To do this he needs to take back his own energy bound up in his previous image of his body as well remove the energy of others connected to it. Here are the questions:

- *Who am I within this body?*
- *What can I do in this body?*
- *Who am I if this body changes?*

The answers to these questions should be different from ten, twenty, or thirty years earlier. Simply examine your beliefs about yourself and the emotions bound up in them. Do you experience yourself as:

- *good-looking, ugly;*
- *masculine, feminine;*
- *healthy, unhealthy;*
- *sexy, boring;*
- *agile, stiff;*
- *tall, small; or*
- *heavy, slim?*

Which emotions do you feel in relation to your replies? Each of these self-attributions can interfere greatly with your perception of reality in the here-and-now.

INTROJECTS OF MATERIAL OBJECTS AND CIRCUMSTANCES

One of Logosynthesis' most interesting discoveries is the fact that not only people, but also material objects or phenomena can form introjects. Joachim, an older participant in a small group at a seminar, neutralised the emotional effects of a car accident three years earlier: the images of the car speeding towards him, the screeching of the brakes, the panic when he was struck.

When he had dissolved these elements of the trauma, he was relieved. He said he would be even more pleased if the pain in his leg were gone as well. He'd had it since the impact of the bumper. As an experiment, I gave him two sentences:

1. *I retrieve all my energy bound up in the bumper of this car and take it back to the right place in my Self.*
2. *I remove all the energy of this bumper from my all of my cells, from my body, and from my personal space, and send it back to wherever it really belongs.*

The experiment proved a success. The pain that had bothered Joachim for three years disappeared within minutes. Two weeks afterwards, Joachim sent me an email thanking me for the seminar. The pain hasn't reappeared.

The incident of Joachim with the car bumper wasn't the only case of a non-human introject. Returning from summer trip by car, I caught a cold because the air-conditioning was too high. I applied Logosynthesis to remove the introject of the current of cold air. My cold disappeared in an instant. At the beginning of the book, I described the case of Fred who had fallen on the root of a tree and broken his arm. Here are some more examples:

- A knife that you've cut yourself with
- The surgeon's scalpel when a wound won't heal after an operation
- The floor you fell on
- The allergens you react to

FINALLY

Logosynthesis offers a broad range of options for dealing with physical symptoms and illnesses. Can it can eventually replace medical intervention? My recommendation: use Logosynthesis to complement and support the medical treatment you need rather than replace it. Your ability to heal yourself will improve if you're completely dedicated to the healing process in the here-and-now.

4.6.
Bad Habits

We should stop smoking, eat less, play more sports, and watch less television. We have our habits; or rather, our habits have us. The best way to predict what people will do tomorrow is to watch what they're doing today—there's a 99 percent certainty they'll do the same thing tomorrow.

Occasionally, on special dates like New Year's Eve or on our birthday, we feel a desire for self-improvement. Scientists have found that it's a matter of a ritual rather than a true necessity. A few days after their good resolutions, most people continue to do the same as before. We are only likely to make changes when the psychological strain increases—our smoker's cough starts to bother us or the scales move mercilessly towards two hundred pounds. Our efforts generally fail because they're made outside of awareness of Essence. Bad habits normally contain elements of dissociation and introjection:

- Dissociated elements reinforce the world perception of our ego. As a slave to a habit, I know who I am. I am a smoker, a drinker. I'm helpless, and indeed, the addictive pattern originated as an alternative when the true Self had no means of expression. Young people start smoking because they want to belong. Adults start to drink because they don't have the opportunity or skills for constructive dialogue with others. Bad habits and addictions, thus, originate as *state management* designed to cope with challenges in life that we can't otherwise overcome. In addition, damaging habits offer something

positive in their own right because their chemistry—nicotine, sugar, alcohol—temporarily improves our state. This state doesn't last long and can only be sustained by a fresh supply of the addictive substance, like pressing a button. These dissociated states have the advantage of inducing positive feelings. The disadvantage is that they are damaging in the long term.
- Introjected elements are the opposing aspect. Parental messages like, "You really should..." are all too familiar. We're reminded of the obvious disadvantages through slogans on packaging such as "smoking kills" through government bans, and the low success rate among alcoholics and obese people. These introjects are activated annually on special dates. Dissociation will prevent our good intentions on New Year's Eve from succeeding. Certain people will activate parental introjects through doctors—doctors are relatively successful if they tell patients to quit smoking. One third of smokers stop when their doctors tell them to in plain language.

In psychological terms there is no winner in the struggle between introjects and dissociation. The opponents are evenly matched and mirror images of one another. The dissociated states ignore the long-term negative effects of the addictive pattern. They hold negative beliefs such as:

- *I'll never manage to give up.*
- *It's like the work of the Devil. Whenever I try to stop, something bad comes along.*
- *it's like being under remote control.*
- *I feel guilty when I'm drinking.*

They may hold positive beliefs such as:

- *It just does me good to have a cigarette now and again.*
- *It's a thrill to speed along the motorway at 220 kph; the world is already full of limits.*
- *People who can't enjoy their food don't enjoy much else.*
- *When I'm drinking, it makes life a bit easier.*

There are intense but static emotions bound up in bad habits—guilt and shame on the negative side; feeling relaxed, happy, and carefree while intoxicated on the other. Gobbling down one or two Big Macs in McDonalds's will make us feel good for a short while.

LOGOSYNTHESIS AND BAD HABITS

From a Logosynthesis viewpoint, people with bad habits have a world view in which they need the support of those habits. They act from dissociated parts, which stabilise them through eating, drinking, smoking, or reckless behaviour. If they don't, they encounter negative images or memories. The archaic part that manages its stability through the habit meets three types of introjects:

1. Introjects that oppose the habit for rational reasons. The damaging habit threatens relationships, the workplace, health, and finances. These introjects are represented by proponents from the areas of medicine, science, the police, the law, social services, and the institutions providing support in modern society. The media and internet also provide informative material. Here's an example of the latter taken from a New Year's Eve edition of our local newspaper.

Stay sober on New Year's Eve. As a study from Finland showed, there is a significant increase in the figures for alcohol-induced fatalities at New Year. The Finnish people do drink even more on Midsummer's. Nevertheless, the risk of death from alcohol poisoning is 25 percent higher on New Year's than on any other day.

2. Introjects that support addictive behavior. These are based on the principle: Let the others just talk. They don't know what it means to be poor/young/black/gay… Have some fun! We all have at least one person in our family representing type one introjects. People with type two messages compensate for these. What they say can be used to maintain the addictive pattern.
3. Introjects that are the real origin of the habit: parent figures who failed to recognise their children's needs for security, respect, and protection. These introjects are silenced when the addictive pattern is activated.

If the decision to change your behaviour is based only on messages contained in introjects from the first group then you're going out of the frying pan into the fire. In fact, introjects from the second group are activated to try to prevent you from taking action. If you don't obey them, you're considered a spoilsport. The real problem, however, is the activation of the third group of introjects. They reveal the reason why the addictive pattern has been useful to you: to rid yourself of them. Archaic feelings of inadequacy, abandonment, and depression appear and destroy the pleasant feeling initially connected to the positive change.

Logosynthesis gets to the root of these problems. It identifies the sequence of dissociated states and introjects involved. The chief obstacles to changing our behaviour are archaic fragments that make you feel sad, ashamed, anxious, or lonely. They become active as soon as you start to eat or smoke less. Most people attribute this to physical causes, but it makes more sense to understand the physical discomfort and negative feelings as what they are: symptoms of dissociation. If you can perceive them as archaic parts, you can use Logosynthesis to treat them as such. Focus on the most perceptible symptom, give it a rating on the distress scale, and begin with the sentences. For example:

1. *I retrieve all my energy bound up in this nausea and take it back to the right place in my Self.*
2. *I remove all the non-me energy connected to this nausea, from all of my cells, from my body, and from my personal space, and send it back to wherever it belongs.*

Do the same for other emotions such as abandonment, sadness, rage, and fury. If images of significant figures from the past come up in this context, they must all be dissolved. While you're doing this, it's again important to examine the location of these introjects in your personal space before and after applying Logosynthesis. This will allow you to perceive clearly any changes.

POSITIVE EMOTIONS RELATED TO ADDICTIVE PATTERNS

One special area for the applying Logosynthesis is positive emotions associated with the habit. In fact, you need to dissolve both the old negative parts and introjects as well as the false positives—the latter sustain the delusion that you're doing something positive for yourself through the addictive pattern.

It's in the nature of bad habits that our behaviour is harmful to ourselves in the long term, but pleasurable in the short term. Consider these examples: the alcoholic who takes another drink to feel better; the driver who catapults his adrenaline level beyond measure by driving at 190 kph on the motorway; or the shopaholic stockbroker who takes home the latest designer item in every colour. Each of them is getting a pleasurable emotion even if it's only for a few minutes. My American colleague, John Diepold, calls positive feelings like these "elaters." They give us a high before the letdown.

It seems ridiculous, especially the first time you do it, to dissolve a positive experience. Why should I let go of my greatest source of comfort? According to the first axiom of Logosynthesis, however, the reconnection between your Self and the Earth Life System relieves all pain. Only from Essence outwards can you begin to shape your life actively.

During your work with addictive patterns, you can consult the applications in 4.7. There are whole lines of beliefs that you can question—flimsy arguments, which can't justify the continuation of the pattern or stand up in the face of really analytical argument. Furthermore, bad habits associated with a large range of negative emotions. Abandoning your familiar behavioural pattern may give rise to shame, sadness, fear, or fury. People don't give up bad habits instantaneously or easily; each element of dissociation and introjection must be dissolved until the Self has at least 51 percent of the decision-making power.

The first and most important step towards change is the awareness that a great deal of your thoughts and emotions are disconnected from Essence and based on dissociation and introjection. This keeps you from your real life's purpose. A second important insight is that the true Self does not suffer. As soon as you take in or are convinced of this axiom and its deepest implications, your life will be different. Logosynthesis will help you to gain this insight step by step. Keep going!

4.7.
Beliefs

"If you believe you can
Or if you believe you can't
You're right."

– HENRY FORD

BELIEFS

Logosynthesis re-establishes the energy flow between Essence and the world through the manifested Self. In this work, we can focus on thoughts, feelings, and behaviour associated with symptoms. We can also work directly with underlying beliefs and basic positions. Beliefs and basic positions define our internal and external reality. They help us to find our direction in life. They originate when we need to process experiences, but cannot yet think rationally because we're too young or because we're overwhelmed; we take in the unfiltered information from the environment. As we do not possess the sufficient capabilities to process it, the information is distorted. Our conclusions may be irrational, but still more tolerable than chaos and incomprehension.

Beliefs stabilise us in the course of our life history. They can simplify our life or complicate it. Emotions, thoughts, and behaviour patterns originate from underlying beliefs. If you view the world as a source of interesting experiences, you can open yourself to others. If, however, you believe that people are out to get you, your actions will be motivated by fear, aggression, or defensiveness.

BASIC POSITIONS

Our basic positions underlie the beliefs governing our daily lives. They influence each moment of our lives, guiding each action, feeling, and thought. They may or may not be connected to the Self. If basic positions are embedded in the Self, development continues—the life task is fulfilled. A classical example is the position, "I'm OK, you're OK," used in transactional analysis. This basic belief supports the development of the whole person and those around them. Alternatively, basic positions only partly embedded in the Self lead to negative emotions and inhibit growth; they connect being OK with fulfilling conditions:

"You're a good boy if you mow the lawn."

This is useful in completing tasks in the material world. However, beliefs like these cause us to depend on our achievements in the outer world and the recognition of others. They inhibit the development of Self-confidence—in the literal sense.

CHANGING BELIEFS

Each memory in itself comprises elements of feelings, thoughts, and behaviours. If you're suffering because of something you think, you're not in contact with your Self, since the true Self does not suffer. Your negative cognition becomes a case for Logosynthesis—it definitely does not belong to your Self.

There are some specific beliefs that get in the way when you want to change your life. They relate to the impossibility of change itself. Fred Gallo, one of the developers of Energy Psychology, identified a list of negative beliefs that can undermine or inhibit positive change. They relate to the following issues:

- Possibility
- Intention
- Value
- Deserving
- Right
- Loss
- Identity
- Risk
- Time
- Money

The following section outlines cognitions relating to the above issues. It also shows alternative formulations.

POSSIBILITY

I cannot solve this problem.

We think that we don't possess the necessary power, ability, or skill to change our own circumstances. The positive alternative to this cognition is:

I can solve this problem.

INTENTION

I don't want to solve this problem.

This belief often is connected to the assumption that other people should solve the problem by dealing with conflicts or are in situations where they have more resources. Nevertheless, others usually suffer less. So it's better to develop the positive alternative:

I want to solve this problem.

VALUE

I'm not worth it to solve this problem.

We think that we're not worth having the problem solved. Our self-esteem doesn't justify it. We have a low sense of personal worth and do nothing about solving the problem. A positive alternative for this disturbing belief is as follows:

This problem is worth solving.

DESERVING

I don't deserve to solve this problem.

We feel that we haven't achieved enough or put in enough effort for ourselves or other people to solve the problem. Here, the alternative is:

I deserve to solve this problem.

THE RIGHT

I don't have the right to solve the problem.

If a problem causes us suffering and other people can't solve it, we're responsible for the next step. Everyone will benefit from a good resolution. If we take responsibility, everyone will suffer less in the end. Here's the corresponding belief:

I have the right to take control of solving the problem.

LOSS

I'll lose something when I solve this problem.

We feel that we'll lose something important by solving the problem. This shows that we don't realise that there's no greater benefit than re-establishing contact with Essence. In the face of this, any loss is insignificant. The alternative belief is:

What I'll lose is less important than what I'll gain if I solve this problem.

IDENTITY

This problem is part of me.

We think that we wouldn't entirely retain our identity if the problem disappeared from our lives. We're afraid of losing our identity or part of it. Yet we're not aware that Essence endures without dissociated parts and stress. Here is the positive alternative:

I can solve this problem and still be myself.

RISK

I'm taking a risk by solving this problem.

No risk means no change. In fact, solving a problem can result in a new situation that demands that we cope with it. We will have re-established contact with Essence. We'll have freed up the resources that were inaccessible to us from the standpoint of the dissociated parts. These resources are directly available to the here-and-now. They will allow us to assess present risks and possible courses of action. The alternative positive cognition is:

I can assess risks and handle them appropriately.

TIME

I don't have time...

This means that every other activity is more important than putting our energies into solving the problem. We often use the shortage of time as a basic justification. Solving the problem is a lower priority than other activities and we're not convinced that it's important. Here is one possible positive cognition:

I have time for what's important in life.

MONEY

I don't have the money to change this.

We think it's more important to spend money on everything except solving our problem. Being short of money often says something about our priorities—quite often professional counselling in a crisis situation in our marriage or the workplace is less of a priority than a new car or a Caribbean holiday. The positive alternative is:

I have money for what is important in life.

POSITIVE COGNITIONS

The negative cognitions in the previous section can underminet many of our attempts to change. Preoccupation with negative cognitions blocks energy, and we remain caught in a downward spiral. This means that it becomes progressively difficult to recognise and apply positive cognitions. Positive alternatives can open the door to a fresh start. Logosynthesis can help you achieve your goals.

THE VALIDITY OF POSITIVE COGNITIONS

This exercise will help you to find the validity of positive cognitions.

- Focus on a current problem in your life, concerning how you deal with other people, work, health, or money and time.
- Write down your thoughts on this problem in a few words.
- Think about what you have done before to solve the problem.
- Examine the truth or validity of each of the following positive cognitions in solving the problem.
- if you think the sentence is completely true or valid for you, give it a seven. If you think the sentence isn't valid, give it a one, or an appropriate score in between.

Positive cognitions are:

I can solve this problem.

I want to solve this problem.

I'm worth it to solve this problem.

I deserve to solve this problem.

I have the right to solve this problem.

What I'll lose is less important than what I'll gain when

I solve this problem.

I can solve this problem and still be myself.

I can assess risks and handle them appropriately.

I have time for what's important in life.

I have money for what's important in life.

Write down your assessment of the here-and-now before you apply Logosynthesis. Note the score for the various cognitions on a scale of one to seven, adding comments. This will allow you to monitor the process of change.

The scale of validity of positive cognitions was developed by Francine Shapiro, an American psychologist. The scale lets you record the validity of each of your cognitions. It is useful when you're applying Logosynthesis to dissolve blocking convictions or disturbing beliefs. You can apply the scale to the validity of the current situation and the desired state. You can monitor your progress as you move from the Ist to the Soll-Zustand.

If you'd like to change a disturbing belief, begin by reformulating the negative cognition along the lines of your goal. If your position is:

People don't like me.

It will become the sentence:

People like me.

Next, ask yourself how true the sentence "People don't like me" is for you on a scale from one to seven.

The scale begins at one because in the worst of all possible worlds, there'll always be people who don't like you much. A score of seven means you're very strongly convinced that people like you.

Now, examine where the people you sense don't like you are located in your personal space. Where are these images? To the left, to the right, in front of you, or behind you? How far away from you are they? What size are they? Apply Logosynthesis to this belief and repeat the sentences 1 and 2:

1. *I retrieve all my energy, bound up in the belief that people don't like me and take it back to the right place in my Self.*
2. *I remove all non-me energy connected to the belief that people don't like me from all of my cells, from my body, and from my personal space, and send it back to wherever it belongs.*

Let the sentences sink in and observe the effect. Examine how the figures change in your personal space and how you react towards them now. Now go back to the score on the scale of positive validity. Has it changed? Many people report that their score on the SUD scale decreases and the score on the validity of the positive cognition increases.

FINDING BELIEFS

Disturbing beliefs and cognitions are seldom formulated clearly. They underlie everyday feelings and thoughts. It takes detective work to discover them:

If a belief were the cause of this problem, what would it be?

If your problem is that you're feeling low because a rival got the job you wanted, the following questions will help you discover the underlying beliefs:

1. *What do I think about myself now?*
2. *What do I think about my colleague now?*
3. *What do I think about life now?*

Note your answers. Examine these thoughts and ask yourself how long these have been familiar patterns. Possible answers are:

1. *I'm a loser.*
2. *Other people always come out on top.*
3. *Life is unfair.*

Such beliefs can harm your self-confidence and professional life if you retain them.

CHANGING BELIEFS

Beliefs are connected to dissociated parts and introjects. As son as you've identified a belief, you can apply Logosynthesis—regardless of the content. Every conclusion and every disturbing belief is an energy construct that has been disconnected from the here-and-now and from your Self. The sentences used in Logosynthesis will dissolve these energy constructs. The following is an example of how to dissolve disturbing beliefs:

- Use the following sentence to initiate the start-up procedure

I activate my Essence for my development in this process.

- Find a situation, feeling, thought, or pattern of behaviour you find upsetting.
- Explore your ideas on the problem with regard to three issues: yourself, other people, and the quality of life.
- Write down these thoughts.
- Begin with the cognition concerning yourself and use the other two as a check. They usually change when the first cognition does.
- Examine where these thoughts or beliefs are located in your body or in your personal space and ask yourself:

  Where is it located or where does it come from? In front? Behind? To the left? To the right? Above? Below? Do I see or rather hear it inwardly?

- Find the positive form of the cognition and estimate its validity on a scale from one (not valid) to seven (very valid). Take note of the issue and values.
- Say the sentences:

  1. *I retrieve all my energy bound up in belief X back to the right place in my Self.*
  2. *I remove all the non-me energy connected to belief X from all of my cells, from my body, and from my personal space, and send it back to wherever it belongs.*
- Let the sentences sink in.
- Re-estimate the validity of the positive cognition.

When applying Logosynthesis to disturbing beliefs, you'll probably have to process a seemingly endless list of ever-changing issues. That's not easy. Keep going!

BELIEFS COME BEFORE EMOTIONS: THE CASE OF REBECCA

Work with beliefs will sometimes help to overcome blocks in applying Logosynthesis. During psychotherapy, a sixty-three-year-old woman learned how to apply the sentences herself and did very well. One day, she couldn't manage. She described to me her fear that her son would be sent to prison. Whenever she read about a robbery, murder, or rape in the newspaper, she imagined that her forty-year-old son could have committed the crime and pictured him behind bars. She'd tried several times to retrieve her energy from this fear. Even after several attempts, she couldn't manage it. This led her to introduce the issue during her session with me.

My experience in similar situations tells me that there's no point in working with the emotions; she'd already tried that herself. So, I tried, along with her, to discover what beliefs were at the root of the fear and mental image of prison. After we had discussed it, we arrived at the sentence: "My son is a potential criminal."

When I asked Rebecca where this belief was located in her personal space, she replied, "Across the whole room, above me." Then she paused for a moment. She said, "It's a guillotine...it looms over me," and she started to cry.

I gave her a sentence to retrieve her energy from the image of the guillotine. Following the first application, the image of the guillotine changed into a scroll of parchment rolled up at both ends. On the scroll, there were some barely legible words. After the second application, she imagined the scroll as being quite old and almost falling apart. When I later asked her to remove the non-her energy from the parchment there followed a strong air current that swept it away, high above the Rhine Valley. Afterwards, the fear that her son could commit a crime had completely left her.

4.8.
The Courage to Take Action

"You've got to search for the hero inside yourself
Search for the secrets you hide
Search for the hero inside yourself
Until you find the key to your life."

– M PEOPLE-BIZARRE FRUIT

There's a difference between desires, plans, talk, and the courage to get into action. At the end of the day, it depends on how we act, whether we show what we can do and what we consider to be our purpose in life. We frustrate ourselves by simply talking and making plans without seeing them through, while we gain courage by taking active responsibility. Unfulfilled desires are always made up of the same things. This will become immediately clear when you ask yourself:

- *Am I ready to take on risks?*
- *Am I happy to change something in my life to realise my goals and tasks?*
- *Am I prepared to take responsibility for my new situation when I've achieved my goals?*

Your replies to these questions say something about an important quality: courage. Courage is the state in life that enables us to take up challenges and pursue our goals without or despite our fear. On close observation, very few people describe themselves as courageous—they either are, or they aren't. Courage is a quality that we attribute to others. To courageous people, their actions are self-explanatory: the Self considers the various factors in the situation, assesses the risks, and proceeds to act.

ASSESSING THE RISK

Realising our personal goals often means change: changing our political beliefs; moving houses; getting married or separated; changing our job or advancing our career; making a financial investment. What do you really want to change? Are you happy to accept the risks attached to these changes?

A risk is invariably accompanied by fear or lack of certainty. You need courage, self-confidence, to face the unknown. Courage is the capability to approach something new, knowing that it's right and appropriate for you to change your situation. You'll only know that if you're in contact with your Self and Essence. How can you achieve this?

- Clarify your goals in the various areas of your life. Most of us alternate between wanting to hold onto something and wanting to change it. Wanting to keep your home or children's school can hold you back from accepting a better job. That's fine in itself. You just need to make a decision and then organise your life around it.

- Formulate your goals clearly. The more specific you are about your goals the easier it will be to assess their impact on your life. It will also be easier to make plans and see opportunities around you to put them into effect.
- List your goals and tasks in order of priority. Every real priority generates a conflict of interests: a long-held desire for a change of job may disappear at the prospect of the financial loss incurred in the more attractive position; a three-month tour in Amazonia may conflict with the desire for a new car.
- Consider the various aspects involved in realising your goal. There's a first step on every journey, and after the first there'll be many more.
- After this process, the belief must still be there that these are your own goals at the most profound level of your existence. If not, other priorities play a role.

When each of these criteria has been fulfilled, your Self will guide your process, and nothing can stop you. You will know that the projected change is the best thing that can happen to you.

LOGOSYNTHESIS AND ASSESSING THE RISK

For a great many of us, calculating a risk activates archaic fragments and introjects. Catastrophic scenarios are set in motion, fantasies are created, and beliefs about our own identity are relived. Memories of injury and abandonment come up, and failure is pre-programmed. Archaic imprints reawaken earlier emotions. They won't give you the resources you need for a fresh start. That's why it's very advisable to keep a record of old images and memories like these, as well as the associated emotions and physical symptoms while you're assessing the risk. You can't look forward to something new, or assess any risk in the present if you're being controlled by feelings that go back thirty or forty years, or even further.

Take a break if you notice that archaic remnants are activated. Apply Logosynthesis to the obstacles blocking your thoughts and emotions as well as early memories that diminish your efforts. If then your analysis has the same result, at least you'll know it wasn't really a good idea to spend resources on it.

MAKING A DECISION

Estimating a risk is one thing; the decision to take a new direction and pursue it is another. A major, planned decision is executed in countless small steps. If you want to study a new subject, you'll have decided to expend time, money, and energy on it. From that point, you have to decide, on a practical day-to-day basis, which activities you'll cancel to have the spare time and balance the books. If you want to lose weight, decide on your desired weight and choose a diet or a strategy. From then on, with every mouthful on your plate, you have to decide whether you actually want to take it up on your fork—a never-ending series of minor decisions.

Tune your decisions to Essence and your Self. The more your Self has been freed from bound energy, the more powerful it will become, and the less influence imprints and dissociated parts will have. Many decisions are modified by the influence of strong imprints. When our Self has lost control, strong imprints can activate adapted parts as well as conflicting ones.

LOGOSYNTHESIS AND DECISIONS

Logosynthesis is not only useful during preparation and assessment, but equally during the implementation stage. Surprisingly, carrying out the decision becomes a great deal easier. The more imprints and parts that are dissolved, the easier it becomes to identify our own long-term goals. The Self gains power over momentary impulses. You may experience the temptation to have another cigarette, take a drink, put a second helping on our plate, or go outdoors in good weather instead of studying. More and more, decisions are unconsciously made in accordance with our goal, guided by our Self.

Logosynthesis can play an important role in these stages. You think of your major, planned decision and realise there are problems in putting it them into effect. You'd rather follow previous patterns in making the small, day-to-day decisions and do everything forbidden by the good counsellor from the beginning of the book.

Logosynthesis will help you to pursue the path to your goal. To achieve this, you need to recognise and admit the inclination to leave your chosen path. The temptation may be a second helping, a cigarette with your coffee, an "interesting" television programme, or because the waiter asks if you'd like anything else. Use the sentences, for example:

1. *I retrieve all my energy bound up in this craving for chocolate and send it back to the right place in my Self.*
2. *I remove all non-me energy connected to this craving for chocolate from my cells, from my body, and from my personal space, and send it back to wherever it belongs.*

Over time, applying Logosynthesis to the process will become your basic attitude. You will make the decision that you no longer want to be controlled by this habitual pattern, but by the higher authority that's always there—your Self.

You'll be increasingly quick to notice when you're drifting off course and will dissolve the corresponding frozen worlds. You'll find it progressively easier to identify what is truly meaningful for you. Essence will take control from the ever-changing alliances of archaic parts and introjects. What initially seemed like an unusual game will soon become a serious matter. It's a great deal more satisfying to run your own life rather than play a series of patterns—familiar, but not really satisfying.

The risk assessment thus leads to the decision, the decision to the plan, and the plan to the goal. As you approach your goal, you'll notice how much time and energy you had previously invested in sustaining familiar patterns. The word "responsibility" has a new meaning. It's your *response-ability* to the questions that life has put to you. You no longer perceive courage only in the behaviour of others who take their responsibility seriously. Instead, you'll be able to accept compliments on your own courage. You just need to let your own Essence work. It was always there before. Previously, you just weren't aware of it.

YOUR GOAL ACHIEVED

You've carried out your plan; you've realised your goal. In retrospect, you often had to overcome obstacles. Yet it wasn't as difficult as you imagined starting out on the road. Now you can rest on your laurels, pause, and consider your next step on the ladder of life. Be careful—the old, frozen messages are lurking here as well:

- *You can never rest on your laurels.*
- *The Devil finds work for idle hands.*
- *When you're successful, you're not part of the crowd any more.*

Your success means that those around you will be confronted by their own lack of success. The project becomes a source of envy and stimulates competition. These are possibly new to you and, as always with new experiences, you fall back on the tried and tested: your previous parts and introjects.

When it comes to achieving your goals, the seeds of the frozen world are still in your history. Many people who made a fortune live in fear of losing their millions again. In a US survey of rich, poor, and super-rich people, the respondents were asked: *How much money would you need to feel really secure?* Surprisingly, they all gave the same reply: *Twice as much.*

So don't be surprised if you can barely enjoy your success, it's just a next step in your process. You can regain your calm by applying Logosynthesis. The more archaic worlds you dissolve, the more efficient and effective you will be in facing your present situation and fresh challenges. Taking responsibility for your earnings is a major responsibility. Five years after their big win, 70 percent of lotto millionaires are poorer than before. The business world witnesses many seven-day wonders: the founder of a business knew how to build it up but not how to run it. Good fortune can help you achieve affluence, but if you don't maintain what you've got, the cash-box will soon be empty again.

People who have the courage to set goals must have the courage to hold onto what they have achieved and take care of it. It demands equally careful planning as the first two stages described in this chapter—the nice car takes maintenance; the big garden you've longed for for ages involves work; money needs to be invested, not just spent.

Success, especially if it's a major success, will separate you from the majority of the people around you. It results in renewed arguments, challenges, and relationships. You may make the surprising discovery in your new world that some people are envious and even hostile. In this situation, there's a strong temptation to blame other people for your problems and the whole thing can start over.

APPLYING LOGOSYNTHESIS TO YOUR GOAL

If you've achieved your goal and aren't happy, it's probably not advisable to set yourself another goal immediately. By doing this, you might conform to a pattern that would ensure more material possessions, but contribute very little to your self-awareness.

Examine your inner world for archaic feelings such as fear, shame, loneliness, disappointment, and lack of self-confidence. Examine your fantasies about losing your earnings, or other people wanting to make you part with your property. Examine your beliefs that you don't deserve to be successful, to be valued, to make a career, or to acquire property. Examine the messages from the people you related to in your personal space and observe your internal reaction.

Each one of these is a possible area of application of Logosynthesis. If you use it to maintain your success, it can form the basis for the next step in your development. You can dissolve your own old beliefs and those of the companions of your childhood. You can dissolve your emotional reaction to these frozen messages.

In this way, you'll take responsibility for your actions and your life. You won't need to blame anybody, least of all yourself. The power of the Word will give you power over yourself in your situation. You'll find it progressively easy to take effect in your environment and to come to terms with it when you can't. You will live from the Self outwards, and live for yourself. That is the courage to take action.

5.

Improving Your Skills

You are now familiar with the four axioms, the procedure, and some possible applications of Logosynthesis. You've gained basic experience and discovered that Logosynthesis can help you to understand and shape your life in a new way.

The final section of this book will improve your ability to apply Logosynthesis. Along with this, you will learn the use of the finger test to decide when to use which sentence and to determine exactly the length of the pause in the process. I'll also give you some tips about details of the procedure.

5.1.
The Finger Test

During your work with Logosynthesis, you need to monitor your process of change closely. In the chapters on fear and beliefs, you already learned the scales for the Subjective Units of Discomfort and the validity of positive cognitions.

The finger test is a refined instrument for analysing the process. You can apply the finger test to find your priorities in the application, or to fix the length of the pause in the process. Finger tests work on the basis of ideomotor cueing. They will be an important source of information once you've mastered this somewhat unusual technique.

It has long since been recognised that involuntary muscular movements and other physical reflexes can provide information. Pendulums and divining rods can detect such *ideomotor cues*. In hypnotherapy, they are used to get in touch with aspects of the client's unconscious. Applied kinesiology uses similar signals in muscle tests to provide information on the progress of the healing process. The use ideomotor signalling is generally met with a certain scepticism. Once you've overcome such scepticism and gained experience, you'll notice that the finger test can provide a great deal of clear information. However, getting really reliable information demands a true withholding of the ego.

The technique I describe here is just one of many, chosen because of its simplicity. If you've acquired skills in other ideomotor methods, use the one you prefer. To discover your own personal ideomotor cues find a quiet place. Stimulate the circulation in your hands; rub your hands together vigorously; move them about and stretch them. Then put your hands on your knees or on a table. Ask Essence directly for support, and to enable you to use move your finger as a signal. Next, ask for a sign from one of your fingers for "yes." Then wait and pay attention to any physical reaction. Essence will work together with your conscious ego, if you're open to this interaction and prepared to receive the signals Essence sends you. If so, one of your fingers will give an involuntary cue. Watch out for any slight moving, twitching, or tingling in your finger. If you notice such a signal, ask Essence to strengthen it. Keep waiting, and note the reaction from your finger. As soon as you receive a signal, express your thanks and ask Essence to repeat the signal. Repeat the process several times until you're sure how the signal looks and feels. Again, express thanks. Then, ask Essence for a signal for "no." Ask Essence again to strengthen the signal and once again express thanks. Once you've found cues for yes and no, the same method will show you signals for "don't know" and "no answer."

Now put your new skills into practice. Use true statements such as, "The grass is green," or "I'm a man/woman" to check if you get a "yes" answer. Then you do the same with untrue statements like "The grass is orange" or "I'm a man/woman" until your finger reacts immediately and independently. Practice usually takes time. Detach yourself from the outcome of the test, observing the movements and feelings in your fingers as if they were somebody else's. Wait, and give the process in your fingers time to advance. Learn to perceive increasingly subtle signals until the movements of your fingers become totally involuntary. Like many people, you may be impatient at the start. You can apply Logosynthesis for this impatience.

When you've learnt how to get a reliable response to true and false statements, you can start to ask Essence for information. Go to your quiet place and place your hands in a relaxed position on your knees or on a table. Phrase your questions to require a yes or no answer, for example:

- *Can I apply Logosynthesis to this symptom?*
- *Do I start with sentence 1?*
- *Do I start with sentence 2?*
- *Do I need to wait longer before I move on to the next stage in the process?*
- *Do I need to repeat the sentence?*
- *In this case, do I need to dissolve imprints as well?*

Your attitude and presence should be quiet and neutral when you ask questions. Stay in a calmly attentive frame of mind while you absorb the information. Keep your scepticism in check for a quarter of an hour and allow your Self to receive answers that the mind doesn't like to hear. It may not understand them or they may not conform to your earlier view of people and the world. The mind can recognise the answer only through the ideomotor signal. It has virtually no access to the information provided by Essence through the finger test. Especially in the beginning, this will lead to doubt and scepticism. Usually such doubts come from physicist, biologist, and psychologist introjects, who tell you that this doesn't make sense and that you're cheating. Resolve these introjects and practice. Once you've learned that the signals are consistent and reliable, you will start to trust the technique and use it.

If an answer seems confusing, ask for clarification. Essence is infinitely patient. If you receive inconsistent answers to a question, interrupt the sequence and return to your meditative attitude. You can recheck everything, all the time. Your awareness of ideomotor signals will be an important source of information on your journey towards personal development and self-healing. You do have other sources of information on your internal processes:

- Your current and previous emotions
- Your thoughts and beliefs, both past and present
- Your dreams
- Your fantasies
- Your body language and nonverbal communication

Sometimes, information from these different sources is not coherent. Ideomotor signals are an additional instrument for finding or verifying information. If you're open to what Essence tells you, this information will be more true than what you can discover by other means. Give yourself time. Logosynthesis works beyond the conscious ego. Your Self has no interest in obscuring or distorting the information from Essence.

5.2.

Tips and Tricks

INTRODUCTION

This chapter contains a number of reflections on the application of Logosynthesis. When you start to work with the model, you'll notice that the method seems simple. You'll also remark that a great many aspects arise, previously of no concern to you, when you were caught in archaic parts. During the early stages, you will focus on the correct application of the method. You'll soon sense that there's more to it. When the true Self fills your consciousness, it will have consequences for your entire existence—for your life as an individual, in relationships, and in your professional life.

You will know more clearly what you want. However, this also means that you need to weigh up when to pursue your interests and when to abandon them. In society, when you no longer refrain from speaking, you need to learn when to speak and when it's better to say nothing.

THE PREPARATION: CHOPPING UP THE SALAMI

If you want to use Logosynthesis to work on yourself, make sure that you won't be disturbed. Start with minor issues and without stress. Go on until the process is engraved in your memory and you can formulate the sentences with ease and elegance.

Focus clearly on the issue at hand before saying the sentences. Be specific: do you want to work on emotions, distressing thoughts, beliefs, or physical symptoms? The more precisely an issue is formulated in the sentences the easier it will be to activate the manifesting power of the Word. In addition, it will be easier for your normal waking consciousness to comprehend the changes you have initiated. When you choose a larger issue to work with, you're unlikely to notice any effect after one or two sessions. Alternatively, if you treat a depressive condition piece by piece, breaking it down into parts like "a resistance to getting up," "the reluctance to call a friend," or "blocks in settling bills," you'll notice the effects of Logosynthesis a lot more easily.

Any other major problem can be broken down into a number of small parts—the salami principle. If you're eating salami, you cut the sausage in slices beforehand; a mouthful of the whole thing would cost you your teeth and you wouldn't enjoy it. We assume that big problems consist of many smaller issues, which can be approached and resolved individually. The more concrete the issue that you apply the sentence to, the better your chance of success. Start with an issue relating to an actual person in an actual context of space and time. You might have felt embarrassed in front of your friend because the meal you'd invited them to last Tuesday was a complete flop. This memory is stored in a split-off part of your Self. Break down the situation into its individual parts and find where the most important aspects came from: was it your guest's face as he tasted your well-intentioned version of a *gazpacho andaluz*? Was it the somewhat icy conversation at some point that evening? Was it the rather formal goodbye kiss? Any one of these factors could be used as the starting point for the Logosynthesis procedure. You can process them one by one until you realise that you've done the best you could and that the evening with your friend needn't necessarily be your last date.

START SMALL AND PRACTICE

In the beginning, choose issues that don't put you at risk of being overwhelmed by intense feelings. It's like flying in a simulator—you familiarise yourself with the different stages of flying and practise them. When the time has come for take-off, every handle is under control. The newly-trained pilot knows his dials and no storm will put him off course. In Logosynthesis, these thunderstorms are the traumas from our past. During your practice sessions, you'll experience the power of the Word and learn how to detect minor changes in your internal state and heighten your awareness. The more you practise, the more deeply your brain will store the nitty-gritty of Logosynthesis. Through repeated application, the procedure becomes automated, and you can get down to work on the thunderstorms.

FORMING SENTENCES

If you're working with a complex issue, the sentences may possibly be very long, for example:

I retrieve all my energy bound up with getting annoyed with my mother at the concert last Saturday back to the right place in my Self.

Many sentences are too long to be said all at once. Your normal conscious mind loses the thread and interrupts the healing process by beginning to establish rules for dealing with such a long sentence. In contrast, your Self will have no difficulty in beginning and processing any sentence, however complex or long. It's best, therefore, to write out long sentences like those below and read them in stages from a piece of paper or from your computer screen:

I retrieve all my energy
bound up with getting annoyed at my mother
at the concert last Saturday
and take it back to the right place in my Self.

and for sentence 2:

I remove all non-me energy
connected to getting annoyed with my mother
at the concert last Saturday
from my cells, from my body,
and from my personal space,
and send it back where it belongs.

MY ENERGY AND NON-ME ENERGY

How many of us take full possession of the symptoms bothering us? Notice how individuals talk about their illnesses:

- *My migraine's come on again.*
- *I had my third heart attack.*

- *My cancer is further advanced.*
- *My eczema's flared up again.*

This connects your symptoms and illness to your identity, and that makes it difficult to get rid of them. You have to separate your symptoms from your Self, otherwise it's a serious breach of Axiom 1: your true Self doesn't suffer. Every application of Logosynthesis must comply with the four axioms. Beginners often use sentences like:

I retrieve all my energy bound up in my headache and take it back to the right place in my Self.

How can you get rid of something of which you claim is yours? So you would be better to say:

1. *I retrieve all my energy bound up with this headache to the right place in my Self.*
2. *I remove all non-me energy associated with this headache from all of my cells, from my body, and from my personal space, and send it back wherever it belongs.*

So, avoid sticking to any symptom by making it your own.

A similar confusion can reduce the effectiveness of the removal sentence. Don't remove your own energy, as in:

I remove all my energy connected to X and send it back where it belongs.

Doing this, you will create a new split instead of dissolving an imprint. You would be better to say:

2. *I remove all non-me energy connected to X and sent it back to wherever it belongs.*

RETRIEVAL OR REMOVAL?

Sentence 1 will usually relieve the client's suffering straight away. The healing effect will later be strengthened by the removal of the energy of introjects using sentence 2. If you start with sentence 1, a part of your own power will come back to you immediately. Then it becomes easier to come up for your interests, especially if powerful introjects are involved. If sentence 2 is not immediately effective, try to find and dissolve the beliefs connected to the block.

Logosynthesis clearly separates our own energy from the energy that belongs outside our personal space. The distinction isn't always obvious. During my work with Margot, an experienced doctor, the image of a sweet, smartly dressed young girl came up. My first impression was that it was a archaic fragment of herself. Surprisingly, however, the image only disappeared after Margot removed the non-her energy from it. That little girl was an illusion. In her parents' eyes, their own daughter had been less than perfect. They compared her with the ideal child they would have liked to have. The image had been firmly lodged in Margot's personal space. After the energy of the little girl was sent out into the universe, Margot expressed great relief.

IMPATIENCE

It's natural to feel impatient, especially at the start of your self-coaching through Logosynthesis. The method is unfamiliar and it seems peculiar to simply repeat a sentence and then sit back. People who have experience of meditation or other reflective techniques such as focusing will usually find it easier to engage in the process.

Take care to take enough time for the pause in the process. Everyone progresses at their own pace. Some people will notice an effect in twenty or thirty seconds, whereas others will have to wait for three to five minutes. The effect also varies. Some will obtain a sense of relaxation throughout their body while in others, the muscle groups will relax one by one. Intense emotions may be dissipated or new thoughts may suddenly show up. It's also possible that your perception of your environment will change—it will suddenly become very calm and you'll hear the clock ticking or the birds chirping in the garden.

If you do become impatient during the pause in the process, take this as a starting point for the next cycle. The power of the Word will be reduced as long as you remain preoccupied with impatience. If you tackle this impatience immediately, you will advance your process of development. Say the sentences:

1. *I retrieve all my energy bound up with this impatience and take it back to the right place in my Self.*
2. *I remove all the energy of others connected to this impatience from all of my cells, from my body, and from my personal space, and send it back to wherever it belongs.*

Even for experienced coaches and psychotherapists, the tempo of the pause in the process seems so slow that you may feel the urge to make "helpful" interventions to speed things up. It's not very easy to remain inactive while the Word works, but you might just as well pull the leaves on the plants in your garden to make them grow more quickly!

During the pause in the process, observe like a curious scientist wanting to know everything about the process taking place. What is happening within your body, from top to bottom and from left to right? What are the changes in your thoughts? What are the changes in your emotions?

Many people find it helpful to watch the process take place like a sunset—the colours change continuously, the temperature goes down, the wind rises and you don't feel the slightest inclination to alter or add on anything. The spectacle is perfect as it is. The more experience you gather the more often you'll notice intense relaxation, and relief will occur.

RATIONALISING

During the processing pause, some people feel the urge to think about the content of the sentences and analyse their effect. Especially at the beginning, their thinking is still split off from Essence and the conscious ego still doesn't know the type of change through Logosynthesis. They think that they must have everything under control. Analysing the sentences reduces their effectiveness.

It's best to give these thinking parts an exercise depending on whether you've said sentence 2 or sentence 2. This will deflect the conscious split-off ego. For example, count backwards from thirty-nine to nineteen. Then compare the changes in your feelings and thoughts before and after you said the sentence. Take your time for the process.

THE SENTENCES "DON'T WORK"

I really believe that *"doesn't work"* doesn't exist. You may not notice any effect because you've taken too big a chunk. You may have skipped onto the next issue without realising, or you may not have enough practice in perceiving subtle changes. The sentence always works, but if you can't perceive that, there are a number of possibilities:

- You're giving yourself too little time to allow the sentence to sink in. Say the sentence, relax, and observe the process as you would a cloud passing in the sky. This will stop you thinking about the process. When you use the application on minor issues, you'll perceive an internal change, which will shed new light on the entire issue and surprise you. This is the power of the Word itself. It isn't based on cognitive processing, but on another creative principle not used for this purpose before.
- Next, observe your reactions calmly from a distance. Observe; don't think.
- If you get impatient, repeat the sentence or count backwards from thirty-nine to nineteen.
- If you don't believe that the sentence—or Logosynthesis—works, stop processing the issue. Instead, treat the disturbing beliefs about the effectiveness behind it.

- The most significant obstacle isn't located in the dissociated parts; it's within the introjects, or the other way around. Alternate between sentence 1 and sentence 2. There's no need to take time for reflection between sentences.
- The issue is incorrectly formulated in the sentence. You need to formulate it more accurately. Alternatively, you may need to subdivide the issue and process each aspect individually.
- The sentence takes effect, but you don't notice. Your new state sometimes seems so natural that you forget you ever had a problem. You can hardly understand any more how bad things had been.
- Keep a written record of your progress. Use the Subjective Units of Discomfort and the scales for the validity of positive cognitions. If you have the same score twice on the scale, a four for example, find out the differences between the first four and the second one.

THINKING AND EVALUATING

Many people tend to make inner statements and judgements on the ongoing process, such as, "it's not possible" or "it doesn't make sense." Such thoughts are generated by your mind and get in the way of the process. Your mind doesn't know—cannot know—how Logosynthesis transforms its familiar patterns.

The power of the Word, expressed through the Self, is greater than the ego with its limited mind. The latter continuously perceives only the same energetic constructs. They're necessary in regulating and stabilising the world. The constructs, however, may become inextricable clots of perceptions, thoughts, and emotions, limiting the perception of the real world. Masses like these usually cannot be altered by rational means and Logosynthesis is a suitable technique. So, if a thought disrupts the process for you, take it as a starting point for the next cycle. For example:

> *I retrieve all my energy bound up in the thought "It doesn't make sense," and take it back to the right place in my Self.*

Allow this sentence enough time to sink in again and note the effect closely. Since such statements originate not only from you, say the second sentence as well:

> *I remove all the non-me energy associated with the thought "It doesn't make sense" and send it back where it belongs.*

WITH GOD'S HELP

Many people think it's so unlikely that Logosynthesis can achieve so much simply by repetition of words that seem other-worldly. They consider applying Logosynthesis to be megalomania or even blasphemy.

In this light, it's difficult to convey that this is not the aim, and that Logosynthesis seeks to re-establish the connection with a higher power. For these people, it can be helpful to amend the sentences using the words "with God's help." The sentences change to:

1. *I retrieve all my energy bound up in issue X, and with God's help, take it back to the right place in my Self.*
2. *I remove all the non-me energy associated with issue X from all of my cells, from all of my body, and from my personal space, and send it, with God's help, back to wherever it belongs.*

This turns the application of Logosynthesis into prayer. And is prayer not the oldest enactment of the power of the Word?

5.3.
The Deeper Process

PAINFUL AND UNPLEASANT FEELINGS

Especially in the beginning, feelings, like thoughts, can get in the way of the application of Logosynthesis. A lot of people tend to consider their familiar emotions as the highest form of reality—they've been there in the same constellations and patterns for years. Their sadness has always been the same; their shame has been the same; their fear, annoyance, jealousy, and greed have been the same. These emotions are like little, dissociated planets that people travel to when a particular thing occurs in their environment. No doubt you'll be familiar with the book *The Little Prince* by Antoine de St. Exupéry. At the beginning of his journey through the universe, the little prince finds himself near asteroids 325, 326, 327, 328, 329, and 330, and he decides to visit them one by one. On each little planet, he meets a man with a frozen life pattern. These men want him to take part in confirming their patterns with them: the king sees him as a potential subject; the businessman perceives a customer or competitor. The little prince doesn't take part, however. He is just surprised that people would live in such a restricted world and continues his journey.

Before and during the application, it makes sense to realise that your intensive emotions are probably just frozen energy patterns, even though they don't feel like that. After the application of Logosynthesis, the world will look different. Then it's important to think about the future. One woman used Logosynthesis to dissolve her anxiety about an upcoming written exam. Suddenly she was confronted with the need to improve her grammar and syntax. This was a question she had never previously considered, because in her fear of the exam regulations, she was paralysed like the rabbit by a snake.

FANTASIES

Unconscious fantasies involving the results of an actual accident are an aspect not to be ignored during your preparation.

Sylvia, a participant at one of our seminars, was troubled by intense, undefined anger. When we spoke, it emerged that as a child she'd fallen through the glass roof of a conservatory. She could see herself lying on the floor among the fragments of broken glass. She had blood on her knee and started to cry. We worked with the different elements of the story: the blood on her knee; the sound of breaking glass; her feeling of terror. In dealing with these aspects, Sylvia's fear remained. I wondered whether we had come to a dead end in our work, as seemed was becoming more apparent. When I asked Sylvia to tell me more, the mystery was solved. When she was lying between the fragments of glass, her mother rushed in, saw what had happened and exclaimed, "Oh, Sylvie. You could have been killed!" At that moment, little Sylvia had begun to imagine how it would look. She could see an image of herself, deathly pale in a coffin, at the front of the church, with her mother in deep mourning. The image depressed her so much that she developed an intense fear of death manifesting itself as unfocused fear in Sylvia's life thirty years later. When we had dissolved this frozen world, her fear subsequently left her.

In processing traumatic events, you're not only going through what actually happened, but also you work with the fantasies associated with them. In your brain's information processing and your energy system, it's irrelevant whether an event happened in reality or in fantasy. A frozen world is a frozen world—an obscure mixture of memories, thoughts, images, feelings, and fantasy. Imprints and dissociated parts often have such a significant effect, because they're impossible to understand rationally. Their content has no real relevance in our work with Logosynthesis. We're aware that recurring thoughts and feelings are empty energetic constructs, like horror films that we can put into the tray of a DVD-player at any time. They only have an effect on us when we watch them on the screen. When we press the stop button, the terrifying spectacle ends.

Logosynthesis is more than just a stop button. It takes the entire DVD of the distressing past out of our system and disposes of it along with the fantasies concerned. However, any information relevant to the here-and-now will be available whenever we need it. After applying Logosynthesis, we can perceive the world in the here-and-now, the world as it really is, unobscured by images from a history now behind us. The fascinating thing about Logosynthesis is that we don't have to *do* anything to dissolve the energetic constructs.

It's enough to say and repeat the sentences as we'd press the eject button on the DVD-player. The DVD no longer affects us, and we can pick up the cover in our hand without pain.

FEAR OF LOSING ANGELS

The poet Rainer Maria Rilke discontinued his psychoanalysis because he was concerned that it would "drive out not just his devil but his angels as well and make him lose his creativity." Some people need suffering to feel the difference from their really good times. To a certain degree, Rilke's statement holds true for Logosynthesis. Memories no longer hold terror; our prevailing mood fluctuates less. The eternal internal dialogue is silenced. This takes getting used to. Some people worry about not being lively anymore, because they're quiet. They're not aware that liveliness can take other forms apart from a permanent exchange of blows between imprints and dissociated parts. If the stillness seems threatening to you, it's a reason to continue with Logosynthesis, not to give up and go on living with the old patterns.

THE SELF AND THE EGO:

Some people ask,

"Can I really pull myself out of the quagmire by the hair? It's almost too good to be true."

The question points towards a misunderstanding about the nature of the ego and the Self. It contains a dissociation.

When you say, "Can I pull myself out of the quagmire by the hair?" you're dividing yourself into an "I" and a "me." In Logosynthesis, you're working from your deeper, your real Self. With the sentences, you're bypassing the ego, which is always focused on this world, with its desires to survive and achieve. Essence, manifesting as our Self, chose this life for a higher purpose. Only the Self has the power of the Word. The mind cannot access this potential because it's caught in polarities it needs to understand the world. The mind can only allow the process to take effect or obstruct it. It's the Self that pulls the ego out of the quagmire of dissociation and introjection. So allow your Self to do the work and observe calmly.

5.4.
Obstacles

I'm not promising you a rose garden or a landscape that will bloom instantly if you make room for Logosynthesis in your life. You should be prepared to encounter obstacles. Nevertheless, we've collected so much experience with the model and the method that we're able to describe these obstacles quite accurately. At the beginning of the book, I asked you to set aside your ideas on change and development until you got to page one hundred. In the meantime, you will have gained some experience of the power of the Word by working your way through this book. You will also have discovered that this power is sometimes evident and sometimes barely noticeable.

Logosynthesis is effective whether you believe in it or not. It will work better and more quickly if your mind doesn't block the process; Essence does the work through the power of the Word and you can observe the results. We can reduce the effectiveness of Logosynthesis in different ways. This chapter outlines some of the recognised obstacles. They erect barriers to the effective and effortless application of Logosynthesis. Some of these obstacles have been dealt with already. They are summarised and defined below:

- Dehydration
- Blocking the power of the Word
- Resistance to the model
- A fear of giving up familiar emotional patterns
- Blocking beliefs about yourself

- A fear of losing life experience
- Missing the deepest cause
- A lack of skills in the new situation
- Assuming that emotions are unique
- Intense emotions
- A sense of emptiness
- Tiredness and exhaustion
- Excessive demands
- After-effects
- The spiral

DEHYDRATION

Working with Logosynthesis initiates an intensive process of change. In Applied Kinesiology, it is recognised that the body needs an increased supply of water during physical, emotional, and mental change processes. If you get a headache during the work or if you feel tired, dizzy, or even confused, drink a glass of water, followed by several litres during the day. The water will support the process and stabilise the results. The application of Logosynthesis will be better integrated on the physical and mental level.

RESISTANCE TO THE MODEL

The model and method of Logosynthesis are new. Many people will identify with individual axioms from this book. They won't agree, however, that it's precisely the combination of the four axioms that is able to dissolve frozen worlds in the shortest time. People look for certainty in their convictions. The history of science shows how the simplest ideas are usually the last to become evident. The best-known example that remains concerns the movement of the planets—it is much more easily explained if we acknowledge that the earth revolves around the sun. In Ptolemy's model of the world, the sun revolved around the earth. For the model to be viable, the planets had to orbit in complex spiral patterns—epicycles—instead of the elliptical courses we know now. Many beliefs about change based on psychological theories for learning and development have a similar complexity. In Logosynthesis, this complexity is unnecessary.

If you don't agree with the model, you must decide whether your image of the world is more important than your distress. Unfortunately, chances are that you'll decide in favour of your image of the world. I recommend you to be pragmatic; sum up all your beliefs about Logosynthesis in one simple sentence and retrieve your energy from it. Next, remove the energy from the introjects questioning Logosynthesis from your system.

Others try to do something to reinforce the effect of Logosynthesis. They may try, for example, to emphasise the sentences or maybe visualise their possible effect. From our overall cultural perspective, it's inconceivable that words can lead to change if, and only if, they are spoken. Alteration or exaggeration is an attempt by the conscious ego to exercise control instead of allowing Essence to take effect. The very words focus and demonstrate, however, the creative power. Any conscious interference with this power diminishes its effectiveness.

FEAR OF GIVING UP FAMILIAR EMOTIONS

We think we know ourselves through our emotions. Some of us even think we *are* our emotions. We're not. Our emotions are a way to stay in touch with our environment, an early warning system to tell us what's going on around us. Many of our emotions have lost that function. They are not a reaction to the actual here-and-now, but have become stable energetic constructs with the purpose of helping the ego predict what's going to happen. They're triggered by introjects activated by environmental stimuli in the here-and-now. Simply take a look at your prevalent emotions:

- *Are you more easily provoked than disappointed?*
- *Is it easier to make you sad than angry?*
- *Is it easier for you to blush with embarrassment than give as good as you get?*

If one comes to you more readily than the others, then it's probably been so for years. So, this is the best time to examine these patterns. The same, of course, applies to the reverse. The more daring people of this world are unlikely to read up to this page in the book, however.

BLOCKING BELIEFS

Beliefs can reduce the effectiveness of Logosynthesis. In order to create a stable image of the world people, form beliefs about themselves, other people in their lives and the quality of life. You may be suffering for years because of negative memories or emotions, but stick to the belief that you don't have the power to change them. This belief must be resolved before you can neutralise negative emotions.

Beliefs and convictions are closely associated with your concept of your identity and who you think you are. I now invite you to try a brief exercise to help you discover the beliefs underlying your emotions. Take a few minutes to complete the following sentences without pausing to think. Just write down the answers that come to mind:

1. *I am…*
2. *I am…*
3. *I am…*
4. *I am…*
5. *I am…*
6. *I am…*
7. *I am...*

You now have seven statements about yourself. Now ask yourself:

- *How long have I been thinking of myself in these terms?*
- *Do other people share this opinion?*
- *Who are the people who see me this way comparing me with?*
- *What evidence do I have of the truth of these statements?*

These seven statements have probably been part of your thinking for many years. No doubt, some significant people in your life think the same, and you yourself may have barely examined these assertions about your identity. This is a sufficient basis for applying Logosynthesis using both these sentences:

1. *I retrieve all my energy bound up in the belief about myself that I am X and take it to the right place in my Self.*
2. *I remove all the non-me energy associated with the belief that I am X from all of my cells, all of my body, and from my personal space, and send it to wherever it belongs.*

Let yourself be surprised! By applying Logosynthesis to these sentences, you'll discover a new sense of identity. It is flexible and will let you react to what's actually going on in front of you in the here-and-now, instead of reinforcing archaic patterns.

FEAR OF LOSS OF LIFE EXPERIENCE

In some people, Logosynthesis triggers the fear that they will no longer have access to their life experience if they neutralise painful events. They're afraid that their live will lose its richness if the emotional burden of the past disappears. The opposite is true. Before the application of Logosynthesis, the existing memories of painful events are limited. Some aspects of their past are exaggerated while others are suppressed. People frequently accuse their parents of dominance, abusiveness, or cruelty. After work with the relevant memories, they find that their parents did the best they could, but that they were stressed or powerless in dealing with their children and other demands in life. The frozen life experience of the child is then completed by a broader, adult perspective. For the first time, the adult understands the pain of the child as well as the heavy burden of the parents. Their experience expands to provide a new, loving standpoint. Earlier imprints are dissolved, and dissociated parts are reintegrated. The content of both is now available to the Self, giving useful information for the person's life task in the present.

FAILING TO DISCOVER THE DEEPEST CAUSE

Sometimes treatment doesn't work because there is a deeper cause beneath the surface of our conscious mind, a cause that isn't eliminated by treatment of the symptoms. Such a hidden cause must be addressed. I discovered the following approach while preparing for a business convention at our institute. My task was to lead a team of seven experts and sixty trainees during a week-long seminar. Following a change in the weather, I suddenly caught a cold at a very inopportune moment. The cold itself showed no signs of improvement after I had applied sentences one and two to treat it directly. It then occurred to me that the cause of the cold might be hidden, inaccessible to my conscious mind, so I altered the sentences:

1. *I retrieve all my energy bound up in the deepest cause of this cold and take it to the right place in my Self.*
2. *I remove all the non-me energy associated with the deepest cause of this cold from all my cells, from my entire body, and from my personal space and send it to wherever it belongs.*

This relieved my symptoms in a few minutes. The following morning, the cold had disappeared. I had just a slight swelling of the nasal membranes and could concentrate on leading the convention. I've never discovered the hidden cause of the cold, but to be honest I've given it no further thought.

LACK OF SKILLS FOR THE NEW LIFE

In many archaic patterns of thought, feeling, and behaviour, people experience themselves as powerless. Dissolving these patterns leads to taking personal responsibility and to actively shaping one's own life. During the process, however, they may find that they lack particular skills or capabilities. One man realised that he always avoided conflict or conceded to another person's argument. When he dissolved the blocked memories behind the pattern, it became obvious that he didn't have strategies for dealing constructively with conflicts. He needed to take a course in conflict management to learn to express his opinions to get them accepted.

ASSUMING OUR FEELINGS ARE UNIQUE

We tend to think that our feelings are unique and belong only to us. This is not so. Feelings like depression, rage, and indignation especially can easily be triggered, taken from us, or reinforced by other people. How often has it happened that people are interested and impartial at the beginning of a conversation, while shortly after they're aware of the same emotions as the person with whom they're talking? This is the reason I recommend to include the removal sentence if you treat distressing emotions, even if sentence 1 has instantly reduced those emotions. People often think they have achieved a state of total relaxation after sentence 1. It's only after applying sentence 2 that they realize what true relaxation is like.

POWERFUL EMOTIONS

Powerful emotions, resistance, and irrational beliefs point to frozen thought forms from the past. It's often necessary to process highly distressing memories in smaller parts in order to observe the effect of Logosynthesis.

With experience, you'll find it easier to direct the process in dealing with intense negative emotions. In the beginning, it's very important to stay with the sentence. If that's difficult, you can write it down and read it from a piece of paper or the screen. You can repeat the sentence bit by bit and stay with it—your Self can comprehend these segments as complete sentences.

THE EXPERIENCE OF EMPTINESS

Many people report a profound calmness after a cycle. This sense of peace is due to ending the familiar internal dialogue of the mind. This inner silence can also create a frightening sense of emptiness, because it allows memories in earlier developmental stages to surface, memories in which there were no speech, images, or differentiated emotions. The ongoing dialogue between your imprints and archaic parts was somehow familiar—it was even part of your identity. It can be very threatening if the blinding, numbing world of introjects falls away, and the familiar patterns cannot support us anymore. The emptiness uncovers new, unknown frozen worlds from earlier stages of development. Then we must learn to listen to the gentle voice of Essence. The experience of emptiness can lead to another cycle in the process of Logosynthesis. You can retrieve your energy bound up with the emptiness, or identify and consequently dissolve the associated emotions.

It may, however, take some time to get to know your internal voice and vocation and translate them into action in your everyday life. One particular form of emptiness enters when people realise that they have conformed to inner and outer patterns unnecessary for fulfilment in life, but for sources of support and security. Letting go of these patterns also means abandoning what is familiar in favour of a still unknown alternative. During this stage, it may be important to seek the support of a trained professional in counselling, coaching, or psychotherapy.

TIREDNESS OR EXHAUSTION

Logosynthesis does not only lead to a sense of calm and relief. Tiredness and exhaustion also show up. It's as though the distress of many years suddenly comes to the surface. Continue the application even if you consider tiredness to be an agreeable and beneficial feeling. In nine out of ten cases, the tiredness disappears within a few cycles of the procedure.

Relief and exhaustion are very much a part of the process. If an introject has stopped you from taking care of your body, you will probably experience an intense exhaustion after applying Logosynthesis. Here it is important to build in sufficient time to be calm and recover. The feeling of exhaustion after dissolving a recurring introject can often last for days.

OVERLOADING THE MIND

Major changes within a short time can bring about a crisis. Take time to process the insights you have just gained and integrate them into your life. Following a period of intensive work, allow your Self an interval for digestion, in which you sleep a lot and drink a lot of water. Take enough time for personal reflection and talking to other people during this stage—finding new words for the new You. You'll notice changes that have taken place. Some of those changes will also be obvious to your friends. They'll describe you as calmer, more patient, and more spontaneous while your personal strengths remain fully intact.

THE SPIRAL

Not only in Logosynthesis, it has become evident that people continuously meet similar challenges. In the early stages, you may think that nothing has changed. If you look at yourself more closely, you will see that pattern is fairly similar, but will vary in intensity or form. If you previously found it difficult to express your point of view in a small group, the problem will only show up now in front of a large audience.

5.5.

Logosynthesis at a Glance

- Find a quiet place where you won't be disturbed.
- Choose an issue where you'd like your Self to exercise greater influence.
- Select an aspect (X) that you find distressing: an image of person or situation stored in your memory, an inner voice, an emotion, a physical sensation, or a thought about yourself, other people, or the quality of your life.
- Examine where this aspect is located in your body or in your personal space.
- Assess the size, colours, movements, and other qualities of the aspect.
- Assign the distress due to this aspect a value on a scale from zero (no distress) to ten (extreme distress).
- Say sentence 2:

I retrieve all my energy bound up in (event, person, place, image, aspect) X and take it back to the right place in my Self.

- Let the sentence sink in for a few minutes, until you notice a change. Observe the effect on your body, thoughts, internal images, and emotions.
- Examine the changes in your body and in your personal space.
- Compare the distress related to aspect X with your score on the scale. Find a new score.
- Say sentence 2:

I retrieve all non-me energy associated with (event, person, place, image, aspect) X from all of my cells, from my body, and from my personal space, and send it back to wherever it belongs.

- Leave a few minutes for the sentence to sink in and observe the effect on your body, internal images, thoughts, and emotions.
- Examine the changes in your body and your personal space.
- Compare the distress related to aspect X with your score on the scale. Find a new score
- Drink a glass of water.
- Make notes on the progress of the application; the issue, aspects, changes in thoughts, feelings, emotions
- Make notes on the images and voices in your body and in your personal space.
- Imagine your future and examine whether the issue still arises.
- If so, treat the next aspect.
- If not, form an image of the future minus the issue. How does it look?
- Stay with it!

6.
Conclusion

"Yesterday is history
The future is a fantasy
Today is a gift
That's why it's called the present."

– BILL KEANE

WE'RE NOT PERFECT

Everyone's personal history is full of unprocessed events. Life issues vary, and the sentences used in Logosynthesis have varying effects. If we start the work through the iceberg of unprocessed experiences, it slowly starts to melt.

People aren't perfect; they don't need to be. The conscious human mind receives forty million bits of information per second from the environment. However, its hardware and software can process just forty bits of information per second. The gap is enormous. Not only our life experience as a child, but also in our life as an adult, we are filled with experiences we will never be able to understand or come to terms with. These experiences are so numerous that parts of our consciousness will split off and new imprints will be formed until we reach old age. So it's not surprising that monks spend many years meditating to obtain enlightenment—the challenges on the road to being whole are too extensive.

It is, however, worth the effort of travelling the road and getting involved in applying Logosynthesis. The more we free ourselves from past influences, the better we can focus on the people, the tasks, and our goals in the here-and-now. We're also better able to enjoy the present moment. Living Essence motivates and stimulates us more than imitating other people.

It's also beneficial to apply Logosynthesis for your well-being in everyday living. More and more of us are suffering from stress. There are more environment demands than we can mentally and physically process. A lot of information disturbs us and is caught up, unprocessed, in dissociation and introjects. Apply Logosynthesis on a regular basis as a remedy for the large number of minor, unexpressed irritations. There is no such thing as perfect communication with everyone else in this world and there never will be. In time, Logosynthesis will be like tooth cleaning for the soul—your own displaced energy is retrieved and the energetic residue of the stimuli of the day is removed. This will help you remain healthy and dedicate yourself to your task as well as assess and enjoy the present.

A NEW DIRECTION

Your newly activated Self will process relevant information constructively and take the necessary steps to fulfil your own life task...*by itself*. If you retrieve your energy from the archaic parts, all that will remain is an awareness of your living, true Self. This is the dynamic connection between the creative intention of Essence and the Earth Life System in the present. It's neither in the past nor in the future. Real life is no computer programme. It's a dynamic interaction with the here-and-now, not a stereotyped sequence of patterns in thoughts and behaviour. The Self takes the lead in processing the information it receives and uses it to fulfil the life task. Learning, however, never stops. The newly aware Self doesn't always have the language and the skills necessary for fulfilling its task. For this reason, you may need support in following your new direction in life. Take time to talk about implementing what you have learnt with your family and friends. A consultation with a careers consultant, a training course, or psychotherapy can support you in finally running your own life.

LEARNING LOGOSYNTHESIS

The Institute of Logosynthesis is continuously developing the model and method. We train practitioners and trainers. The institute has a homepage and a register of trained practitioners accredited by the institute. If you need professional support while you're reading, or after you've finished, this book, you can contact one of them. If you have certified professional training in coaching, counselling, supervision, or psychotherapy you are eligible to attend the official training programme in Logosynthesis. On our international homepage at www.logosynthesis.net, you'll find information on Logosynthesis in several languages, lists of recommended practitioners and trainers, and reports of the experience as well as additional information on the content of the training programme. You can also order books and DVDs on Logosynthesis.

Institute for Logosynthesis®
Pardellgasse 8a
CH-7304 Maienfeld
+41 81 302 77 03
info@ logosynthesis.net
www.logosynthesis.net

Resources

Almaas, Ali Hameed. 1998. *Essence. The Diamond Approach to Inner Realization*. York Beach, ME: Weiser.

Assagioli, Roberto. 1965. *Psychosynthesis. A Manual of Principles and Technique*. New York: Hobbs, Dormann & Company.

Berne, Eric. 1961. *Transactional Analysis in Psychotherapy*. New York: Grove.

Callahan, Roger J. 1985. *Five Minute Phobia Cure*. Wilmington: Enterprise. (out of print).

Descartes, René, and Ivo Frenzel. 1960. *René Descartes*. Frankfurt/Main: Fischer.

Craig, Gary. 2008. *Emotional Freedom Techniques*. http://www.emofree.com.

Diepold, John H., Britt, Victoria, and Sheila S. Bender. 2007. *Evolving Thought Field Therapy*. New York: Norton.

Frankl, Viktor E. 1987. *Logotherapie und Existenzanalyse. Texte aus fünf Jahrzehnten*. München: Piper.

Gallo, Fred. 2005. *Energy Psychology. Explorations at the Interface of Energy, Cognition, Behavior and Health*. Boca Raton FL: CRC Press.

Goethe, Johann Wolfgang von. 1881. *Faust*. Heilbronn: Henninger.

Hell, Daniel. 2002. *Die Sprache der Seele verstehen. Die Wüstenväter als Therapeuten*. Freiburg: Herder Spektrum.

Kafka, Franz. 1966. *Betrachtungen über Sünde, Leid, Hoffnung und den wahren Weg*. Frankfurt am Main: Suhrkamp.

Lammers, Willem. 2007. *Logosynthesis – Change through the Magic of Words*. Maienfeld, Switzerland: ias.

Patanjali. 1997. *Yoga Sutras*. Trans. Alfred Scheepers. Amsterdam: Olive Press.

Shapiro, Francine. 2001. *Eye Movement Desensitization & Reprocessing. Basic Principles, Protocols and Procedures*. New York: Guildford Press.

Sharma, N.V. 1963. Indische Erziehung. *Pädagogische Rundschau, Monatsschrift für Erziehung und Unterricht*, 10. Ratingen: Alois Henn Verlag.

Tart, Charles T. 2007. What Death Tells us about Life. *Shift at the Frontiers of Consciousness*, 17: 30-35.

Wilber, Ken. 2000. *A Theory of Everything. An Integral Vision for Business, Politics, Science and Spirituality*. Boston: Shambhala.